T0305941

"… a comprehensive look into the history and creative process of contemporary film scoring. A must-read for all lovers of movies and movie music."

Pinar Toprak, Composer of *Captain Marvel* and *Fortnite*

" Although there are a few books dealing with music written for films, there are none that I know of written by an accomplished composer. Kenneth Lampl's book contains numerous entertaining and instructive insights that are absent from other works in this genre."

Bruce Beresford, Director, Academy Award-winning
Driving Miss Daisy and *Breaker Morant*

"More than a how-to guide, and more than an overview of the history of film music, composer and industry insider Kenneth Lampl weaves together the best insights from the best in the business to understand why the soundtrack has come of age."

Dan Golding, Host, *ABC Screen Sounds*

"Kenneth Lampl is a composer as capable of massive sci-fi epics as an intimately twisted psychological thriller. And you can tell that he's more than well versed in all the shades of soundtracks."

Daniel Schweiger, The Film Music Institute

FILM MUSIC

THE BASICS

A comprehensive introduction to film music, this book provides a concise and illuminating summary of the process of film scoring, as well as a succinct overview of the rich history of contemporary film music.

Written in a non-technical style, this book begins by presenting a brief history of film music, covering topics ranging from blockbuster franchises to indie film scores. It explores film music from around the world, including Bollywood and European Avant-garde cinema, and film music in animation, like Disney-Pixar and Japanese anime. It then offers a guide to the language of film-music analysis, the creative process behind composing film music, and the use of current technology. The book champions diversity in the industry, with case studies and interviews from a range of active film composers, including Pinar Toprak (*Captain Marvel*, 2019), Kris Bowers (*Bridgerton*, 2020), Natalie Holt (*Loki*, 2021), and Rachel Portman (*Emma*, 1996).

Complete with a glossary of key terms and further reading, this book is an invaluable resource for all those beginning to study film music, as well as lifelong film-music buffs seeking to update their understanding of film music.

Kenneth Lampl is a professor of music at the Australian National University where he is the convenor of the Composition for Film and Video Games Program. Lampl is also an award-winning film composer who has scored over 100 films including the first two *Pokémon Movies, Frontera, The Furies, 2067*, and *Sissy*.

THE BASICS

For more information about this series, please visit: www.routledge.com/The-Basics/book-series/B

FILM MUSIC

THE BASICS

Kenneth Lampl

Routledge
Taylor & Francis Group

LONDON AND NEW YORK

Designed cover image: @Getty Images

First published 2024
by Routledge
4 Park Square, Milton Park, Abingdon, Oxon OX14 4RN

and by Routledge
605 Third Avenue, New York, NY 10158

Routledge is an imprint of the Taylor & Francis Group, an informa business

© 2024 Kenneth Lampl

British Library Cataloguing-in-Publication Data
A catalogue record for this book is available from the British Library

ISBN: 978-1-032-26746-3 (hbk)
ISBN: 978-1-032-26745-6 (pbk)
ISBN: 978-1-003-28972-2 (ebk)

DOI: 10.4324/9781003289722

Typeset in Bembo
by Apex CoVantage, LLC

CONTENTS

ACKNOWLEDGMENTS

I would like to thank Lucy McClune at Routledge, Taylor & Francis for providing me with an initial opportunity to write about film music. Thank you to everyone else at Routledge, especially Georgia Oman and Payal Bharti, for seeing this book all the way to the end.

I want to also thank my editor, Ryan Pinkard, and my colleagues at the Australian National University who have encouraged me on this journey. My biggest thank you goes to my wife, Maria Filardo, for being there for me both before the writing begins and whenever it ends.

1

THE HISTORY OF FILM
MUSIC IN HOLLYWOOD

THE BEGINNING

When I was a child, I loved going to the movies. There was a special dream-like alchemy that occurred when the lights dimmed, and the images and sound surrounded you. It was like stepping into the cocoon of your own imagination, a place where reality and the laws of physics ended, and a new world of possibility began. It was magic.

> Without John Williams, bikes don't really fly, nor do brooms in Quidditch matches, nor do men in red capes. There is no Force, dinosaurs do not walk the earth. We do not wonder, we do not weep, we do not believe. John, you breathe belief into every film we have made, you take our movies, many of them about our most impossible dreams, and through your musical genius you make them real and everlasting for billions and billions of people. – Steven Spielberg[1]
>
> I think that over the centuries we are compelled to tell stories, compelled to make up stories and that's what film is about: we're compelled to tell the fable of our existence, of our human journey. And I think when we run out of words, and when we run out of beautiful pictures, we have to resort to this other language called music. – Hans Zimmer[2]

EDISON KINETOPHONE

The history of film music is also the history of sound in film. Thus, our story begins with one of the original American pioneers of film: the prolific inventor Thomas Edison. Though Edison didn't invent motion pictures, he did invent the phonograph in 1877, a device that could record and playback sound etched onto a wax cylinder. In February of 1888, Edison attended a lecture by motion photographer Eadweard Muybridge, the man who first recorded the moving gait of a galloping horse, and the inventor of a very

DOI: 10.4324/9781003289722-1

crude projector device called the *zoopraxiscope*. The zoopraxiscope was a lantern Muybridge developed that projected images in rapid succession onto a screen from photographs printed on a rotating glass disc, producing the illusion of moving pictures.

Afterward, the two men met privately. Edison thought, *Why not marry a sound recording with the moving pictures of Muybridge's zoopraxiscope?* There was just one major technological hurdle: there was no way of amplifying the sound of the phonograph for large audiences to hear. Because of this problem, Muybridge abandoned the idea and returned to photographing his motion studies, but not Edison. In 1894, Edison and his employee, William Dickson, experimented with recording sound and images together, resulting in a playback device called a *kinetophone*, which was essentially a kinetoscope – another early film-viewing device – connected to a phonograph by two headphones. The first syncing of recorded sound and image was born.

THE SILENT ERA

During the Silent Era, when the first moving pictures were created, the medium quickly evolved from a personal viewing novelty into a public and artistic form of storytelling, similar to other narrative art forms, such as opera. For fledgling filmmakers and audiences alike, it became apparent that the theaters were missing something, and that something was music. Without the widespread technology to synchronize sound with moving images, film remained a photographic medium at this time. And there was still the problem of how to amplify the sound. How would people view a film with accompanying music? The best solution available at the time was for the music to be performed live. During the Silent Film Era, music was typically provided by a solo piano or organ, a small ensemble of three to ten musicians, or a large symphony orchestra, depending on the size and budget of the theater.

There were two basic types of scores: *improvised compositions* and *compilation compositions*. With improvised film scores, the music was composed spontaneously by a skilled pianist or organist as the movie was playing. Here, the musician merely mirrored the action on the screen. For instance, if something exciting was occurring on the screen, the pianist would play something upbeat and loud. If something sad was occurring on screen, they would play a slow, repetitive piece of music, perhaps in a minor key. Compilation scores, on the other hand, relied on pre-existing material. In the early 20th century, there were countless popular songs and classical pieces that were compiled into large binders containing sketches, outlines, and cheat sheets for playing them. During a movie, piano players and organists would simply choose a piece that reflected what was happening on the screen, then continue to play piece after piece until the film ended. Binders were also made for ensembles of differing sizes, and if the ensemble was large enough, a conductor would select the music to be performed.

THE FIRST FILM SCORE

People are often surprised to learn that Camille Saint-Saëns, the French classical composer of "Danse Macabre" and "Carnival of the Animals," composed the first score written specifically for a film. At a time when the film industry was in its infancy, it was a major coup for the producers of *L'Assassinat du Duc de Guise* (1908) to hire France's most famous composer to write the music for their 15-minute historical drama.

Camille Saint-Saëns, who was 73 years old at the time, was at the pinnacle of his career. He had decades of experience in the grand opera tradition, a growing familiarity with early recording technology, and the finest group of artists ever assembled for a film. Saint-Saëns composed the music scene-by-scene as he watched the film, using French chamber ensemble-style instruments: the flute, oboe, clarinet, bassoon, horn, piano, harmonium, and strings. The music was then performed live in the theater while the film was projected. As striking and innovative as Saint-Saëns' music was, the picture compilation binder continued to dominate nearly all theaters as the preferred choice of musical accompaniment with live performers.

VITAPHONE, *DON JUAN*, AND *THE JAZZ SINGER*

Using a series of 33 1/3 RPM discs – a predecessor to the vinyl records that became the dominant form of music playback by the middle of the 20th century – Western Electric and Bell Telephone Laboratories created a sound-on-disk system called the *Vitaphone*. The Vitaphone system was essentially a combination of a film projector and a record player. At the time of shooting, a film camera would be synchronized with a record-pressing machine. Despite how primitive this system may appear, the end result would be that the film and audio would be recorded at the same time, creating the first synchronization of sound and image. When representatives from Western Electric attempted to sell the technology to Hollywood in 1925, they encountered extreme resistance; none of the major studios believed that sound and music would attract audiences.

Finally, a small studio named Warner Bros. purchased the Vitaphone sound-on-disc system in 1926 and debuted it with the lavish costume drama *Don Juan*, which featured a score performed by the New York Philharmonic Orchestra. The *Don Juan* score consisted of both original music composed by Willam Axt, as well as some pre-existing classical pieces. *Don Juan* was a big success and a major step forward in bringing recorded film music to the public's attention. However, it was Warner's next music-aided movie that would change the course of film history.

The Jazz Singer (1927) was the second Vitaphone feature to be produced by Warner Bros. In *The Jazz Singer*, the performer Al Jolson would stand on stage and lip sync to the pre-recorded tracks. With the iconic and improvised words, "Wait a minute . . . wait a minute . . . you ain't heard nothin' yet," a new era of dialogue and sound was born. Even though only one-fourth of the film was recorded with sound – comprising songs and a few lines of dialogue – the movie was an immediate sensation. Warner Bros. would follow this up with *Lights of New York* (1928), the first feature film in which every line of dialogue was recorded.

Despite the success of these *talkies*, as they were soon called, much of Hollywood predicted that sound was nothing more than a passing novelty. But by the close of 1927, it was becoming increasingly evident that sound was here to stay. It was a dismal year for the industry, with only the sound films attracting major audiences. Even the worst film with sound outsold the best silent film. By the summer of 1928, when *Lights of New York* dominated the box office, every studio in Hollywood possessed a license for an individual sound system. In 1929, three-quarters of all Hollywood films featured some form of pre-recorded sound, including 335 all-dialogue features, while 95 films featured a combination of dialogue and subtitles, and 75 had musical scores and some sound effects.

By 1932, silent film was all but forgotten, while the Vitaphone was supplanted by a new technology, *optical sound*, which could print sound directly onto the film, allowing real dialogue and music to be recorded as the film was being shot. Fox's *Movietone* and RCA's *Photophone* became the optical sound standard in the United States, while Tobis Film's *Tri-Ergon* system was adopted in Europe.

THE GOLDEN AGE OF HOLLYWOOD

OPTICAL SOUND ON FILM

As one of the first devices to record sound directly onto film using an optical sound-on-film track, RCA created the Photophone in 1928. Photographically recording the soundtrack onto the film strip, creating a composite, or *married*, print, all sounds were monophonic and played from a single central speaker, as opposed to stereo (two speakers, left and right), which had yet to be invented.

In order to promote their newly developed technology, RCA formed a film production company called RKO, which quickly became one of the "Big Five" film studios that dominated the early days of Hollywood. RKO produced a number of well-known films, including *Citizen Kane* (1941), *It's a Wonderful Life* (1946), *The Best Years of Our Lives* (1946), and *Oklahoma!* (1955). RKO was also the distributor for the Disney films *Snow White and the Seven Dwarfs* (1937), *Pinocchio* (1940), *Fantasia* (1940), and *Cinderella* (1950).

From the start, the pioneering film company was at the forefront of technological advances in sound and visual effects because of its relationship to its parent tech company RCA, which was itself one of the major American electronics companies of the time. One of RKO's most ambitious projects was the epic tale *King Kong* (1933), which saw one of the first uses of stop-motion animation in a feature Hollywood film. What would go on to be the most important historical contribution of *King Kong* was not the innovative visual effects, but being one of the first films to commission a completely original score. Not only was composer Max Steiner's score a milestone, but it created the template for most of film-scoring techniques still used today.

King Kong

Even with the success of motion pictures with sound, the role of the music was very similar to its use in silent films, in its reliance on popular songs and pre-existing classical pieces. When composers were given the occasional opportunity to write original music for a film, it was mainly as a prelude or postlude over-ture. While the first film with a fully original score was *Symphony of Six Million* (1932) – also produced by RKO and with music composed by Max Steiner – it was *King Kong* that received critical acclaim and widespread attention as a revolutionary moment in film.

Employing a 46-piece orchestra and recorded on three separate tracks (sound effects, dialogue, music), Steiner's groundbreaking score represented a paradigm shift because it was the first major Hollywood film to feature a thematic score, as opposed to background music. *King Kong's* score was crucial to the film because it lent realism, drama, and wonder to a fantastical plot. Of course, the studio's executives were initially skeptical about the need for an original score, but because they disliked the film's unconvincing special effects, they gave Max Steiner permission to attempt enhancing it with music. Steiner utilized a number of innovative film-scoring techniques, such as the use of Wagnerian *leitmotifs* – specific themes for individual characters – and *Mickey Mousing* – music imitating the motions of the characters by precisely imitating their rhythm – two techniques that form the basis of contemporary film scoring. Our most beloved film scores, from *Star Wars* to *James Bond* to *The Lord of the Rings*, utilize the leitmotif technique, while Mickey Mousing laid the groundwork for the compositional approach to animated film music through the meticulous synchronization of music and image.

The fully original score for *King Kong* was a grand experiment and was initially viewed with much skepticism. In Max Steiner's own words:

> *King Kong* was the film that saved RKO from failure. But when it was finished, the producers were skeptical about what kind of public reception they could expect. They thought that the gorilla looked unreal and that the animation was rather primitive. They told me that they were worried about it, but that they had spent so much money making the film there was nothing left over for the music score. . . . But the man who was most responsible for the picture, producer Merian C. Cooper, took me aside and said, 'Maxie, go ahead and score the picture to the best of your ability and don't worry about the cost because I will pay for the orchestra or any extra charges.' His confidence in the film was certainly justified . . . It was made for music. It was the kind of film that allowed you to do anything and everything, from weird chords and dissonances to pretty melodies.[3]

With the success of Max Steiner's *King Kong* score, an original orchestral score became an essential part of all films moving forward. Film studios rushed to hire composers, arrangers, orchestrators, conductors, and orchestral musicians. This ushered in the Golden Age of Hollywood and the studio system that produced such unforgettably scored classics as *The Wizard of Oz* (1939), *Singing in the Rain* (1952), *Ben Hur* (1959), *Rear Window* (1954), *Frankenstein* (1931), and *The Adventures of Robin Hood* (1938).

For his part, Max Steiner continued to have a profound impact on the techniques, approaches, and conventions that continue to form the basis of film composing to this day, earning him the universally recognized title of "father of film music." Between the 1930s and 1960s, his name was attached to such iconic films as *Gone with the Wind* (1939) and *Casablanca* (1942), while earning three Academy Awards for his music in *The Informer* (1935), *Now Voyager* (1942), and *Since You Went Away* (1944).

Steiner's score for *Gone with the Wind* marked another milestone in Hollywood film history. The epic, three-hour tale, set against the backdrop of the Civil War, remains the highest-grossing film in history after accounting for monetary inflation (bigger than *Avatar* (2009), *Titanic* (1997), *Star Wars*, and all the Marvel movies). The momentous score is over two and a half hours of music, which took 12 weeks and five orchestrators to complete. The process of composing a score of such size in that short amount of time exhausted the composer, who recalled:

> We used to start [recording] at 8:00 p.m. at night and finish at 7:00 a.m. in the morning with the orchestra, because in the daytime I had to write. I slept four or five hours, then a doctor would come in about noon to give me a Benzedrine injection so I didn't fall over.[4]

As the film industry began embracing the original orchestral score, studios hired not only full-time professional recording orchestras onto their staff, but teams of composers, conductors, arrangers, orchestrators, and copyists to handle the massive workload. In 1939 alone, 365 films were released – one for every day of the year – with moviegoers buying tickets at a rate of 80 million per week. As a result, many of the great film composers of the day, such as Milos Rosza, Hans Eisler, Dimitri Tiomkin, Erich Korngold, Franz Waxman, Bernard Herrmann, and Elmer Bernstein, found lucrative careers in Hollywood. Furthermore, the studio fostered an apprenticeship system where a young musician could begin as a copyist and rise up the ranks as an orchestrator, then an arranger, and finally a composer. John Williams is one of the very last living composers who was trained through this apprenticeship system.

END OF THE GOLDEN AGE

The Golden Age of Hollywood began to wane in the late 1950s and early 1960s because of two important factors. The first was that, before 1948, the big studios also owned the movie theaters, which provided the distribution of their films. That changed in 1948 when the Supreme Court of the United States ruled that this was an illegal vertical monopoly, which effectively put an end to the studio's mass-production mentality and the classic studio system. The second factor was the introduction of a new household technology: the television. As a result of suburban audiences having to decide between going to the cinema and watching the newest TV show, movie theater attendance dropped by 50 percent between 1946 and 1955.

With the old business model dying, innovative movie producers realized that the only way to get people out of the house was to show them something they couldn't get at home. With the goal of enhancing the cinematic experience, studios began to use stereoscopic 3D, which led to an explosion in widescreen aspect ratios and huge projections, and the introduction of multitrack sound to create an immersive atmosphere. With all previous movies (as well as TV shows) recorded and reproduced using a single mono track, Walt Disney's 1940 music anthology *Fantasia* was the first film to be released in stereo sound.

TRANSITIONAL YEARS

By the mid-1950s, the original Hollywood studio system, which had established film as a major artistic and economic force in American culture, began to dissolve. With this decentralization of stylistic power came a wider diversity of films and, by extension, new approaches to film scoring. Up to this point, the model for the film score was based on the European romantic symphonic tradition established and exemplified by Max Steiner. However, a new generation of directors had new ideas on the role of music and picture, and throughout the 1950s the introduction of jazz, as heard in Alex North's *A Streetcar Named Desire* (1951) and Miles Davis' score to the French noir *Elevator to the Gallows* (1958), became more popular.

The 1950s also saw a rise in the use of songs in dramatic scoring. Sung by country singer and actor Tex Ritter in the opening credits of the 1952 Western *High Noon*, the song "The Ballad of High Noon" (also known as "Do Not Forsake Me, Oh My Darlin'") was the first original song composed for a non-musical film to reach the music charts. From that point on, film producers exerted more pressure on composers to compose popular songs as part of their dramatic scores.

This trend culminated in the 1967 Mike Nichols film *The Graduate*, whose generation-defining soundtrack consisted exclusively of licensed songs, with the exception of Simon & Garfunkel's "Mrs. Robinson," which was written for the film. In its wake, song licensing became an important component of many film scores, a trend that continues today with films like *Guardians of the Galaxy* (2014) and *Baby Driver* (2017), which are written specifically to feature popular songs.

The invention of the synthesizer in the 1960s revolutionized the world of popular music, influencing progressive rock in bands like Pink Floyd, Yes, Emerson, Lake & Palmer, and Genesis. Simultaneously, German krautrock bands such as Kraftwerk, Tangerine Dream, Can, and Neu! were creating a new, heavily synthesized kind of music that would be the precursor to what we now call electronic music. These musical innovations found their way into the sound of motion pictures with fully synthesized scores like Wendy Carlos' music for *A Clockwork Orange* (1971), John Carpenter's score to *Halloween* (1978), and Vangelis' work on *Blade Runner* (1982).

The 1960s and 1970s were a time of great revolution, culturally and musically. The aesthetic of filmmaking had changed from the time of the Golden Age, and its score needed to change as well. The days of the classical European film score had ended, or so we thought before 1977, when John Williams single-handedly revived the sound of the big Hollywood orchestra with his score to *Star Wars*.

STAR WARS

First launching us into a galaxy far, far away back in 1977, the *Star Wars* films and its sequels, prequels, and spin-offs, have thus far grossed $7.8 billion at the global box office, before including a staggering $32 billion for all the merchandise, video games and the *Star Wars: Galaxy's Edge* attraction at Disneyland. Composed by John Williams, the original film's now-iconic soundtrack became one of the highest-selling non-pop records of all time, while helping establish one of the great franchises in movie history.

According to *Star Wars* creator George Lucas:

> About 90 percent of the *Star Wars* films are music. It's done in a very old-fashioned style, as silent films, so that the music kind of tells the story . . . The score is a very, very important element of the success of the movies. Without somebody as brilliant as Johnny doing the scores, I don't think they would have been as successful as they were. . . . It's equal to the script or the cast, easily.[5]

Star Wars fundamentally altered the aesthetics and narratives of Hollywood films, shifting the emphasis from deep, meaningful stories based on dramatic conflict, to expansive, special-effects-laden blockbusters. Prior to *Star Wars*, special effects had not advanced significantly since the 1950s. The original trilogy's commercial success in the late 1970s and early 1980s sparked a boom in cutting-edge special effects.

One of the major technical advancements of *Star Wars* was the innovative Dolby and THX sound playback technology – one of the first examples of surround sound – which was designed specifically for the movie.

In 1975, George Lucas and *Star Wars* producer Gary Kurtz approached Dolby Laboratories to discuss the film's soundtrack. They believed that a film of this nature required a soundtrack of a higher quality than could be achieved with conventional techniques, and from Dolby's perspective, the subject matter would allow them to demonstrate their sound technologies to mass audiences.

Under this partnership, more than half of the first-wave release theaters for *Star Wars* were equipped with Dolby theater playback packages, which included the noise-reduction decoders and equalizers necessary to precisely match the loudspeaker responses of the dubbing theater where the film was mixed. Thus, for the first time ever, the sound heard in the theater was virtually identical to what the director heard during the mixing process, representing a major step towards achieving the high-quality sound reproduction and theater playback that audiences today expect.

As Dolby Director of Content and Creative Relations Stuart Bowling explains:

> Until *Star Wars*, we were working only in stereo, but with surround sound, from that first moment where you get the title crawl, and the Star Destroyer comes in from the

top, audiences felt as if it was coming over them, and they were cheering. It became a game-changer from a technological as well as an audience-experience perspective.[6]

George Lucas concurs, saying:

[Dolby's] pioneering work in sound played a pivotal role in allowing *Star Wars* to be the truly immersive experience I had always dreamed it would be.[7]

JOHN WILLIAMS

One of the all-time great composers, John Williams was born in Queens, New York, in 1932. Growing up surrounded by music – his father was a jazz drummer and percussionist in the CBS radio symphony – he began to learn the piano before picking up the trumpet, trombone, and clarinet, and ultimately studying at the Juilliard School of Music.

Starting his career in Hollywood as a studio pianist on such films as *South Pacific* (1958), *Some Like It Hot* (1959), *West Side Story* (1961), and *To Kill a Mockingbird* (1962), he began composing for television shows like *Wagon Train* (1957–1965), *Lost in Space* (1965–1968), and *Gilligan's Island* (1964–1967), before establishing a reputation as a composer for high-budget disaster films such as *The Poseidon Adventure* (1972), *The Towering Inferno* (1974), and *Earthquake* (1974). In 1974, Steven Spielberg asked Williams to score his first feature film, *The Sugarland Express*, thus beginning their long-lasting partnership on such classics as *Jaws* (1975), *Close Encounters of the Third Kind* (1977), *E. T. the Extra-Terrestrial* (1982), *Schindler's List* (1983), *Saving Private Ryan* (1998), and the *Indiana Jones* and *Jurassic Park* series. With 53 Oscar nominations to his name, he is the second most-nominated person in Academy Award history after Walt Disney.

The music of the *Star Wars* universe employs a wide range of musical styles, many of which are derived from the late-romantic idiom of Richard Strauss and his contemporaries, which were first incorporated into the Golden Age Hollywood scores of Erich Korngold and Max Steiner. Even before involving John Williams, George Lucas knew he wanted to highlight his so-called space opera's underlying fantasy narrative rather than the science fiction setting, grounding the otherwise outlandish setting with familiar, audience-accessible music. As *Star Wars* sound editor Ben Burtt remembers it:

[Lucas] wanted a traditional symphonic score in the tradition of Max Steiner or Eric Wolfgang Korngold. We would take music cues from records like Holst's *The Planets*. I did a lot of that myself. George had picked a few music cues that he had listened to while he was writing the film. It gave him an inspiration for what he wanted to see and hear . . . The whole idea of doing a temp track [reference music tracks used for editing before the score is composed] was important because if you have music in the early version of the film it communicates a lot to the composer. It's easier to put in a cue and say, 'This is the direction I want to go,' than it is to explain it with just words.[8]

George Lucas originally intended to use tracked classical music in a manner similar to Stanley Kubrick's *2001: A Space Odyssey*. As such, John Williams was advised to create a soundtrack with recurring musical themes to enhance the story, while Lucas's selection of music could serve as a temporary track for Williams to base his musical selections on. This led to numerous references or homages to the music of Gustav Holst, William Walton, Sergei Prokofiev, and Igor Stravinsky in the *Star Wars* score.

Lucas said his choice of John Williams for *Star Wars* was largely based on Steven Spielberg's recommendation, recalling:

> I said I was looking for a composer who could write in the classic Hollywood style of the '30s and '40s, and [Steven] said, 'John's the man for you, he's fantastic.' I thought, 'Really? He can really do [Erich Wolfgang] Korngold and [Alfred] Newman and all the classic guys?' And Steven said, 'Oh yeah, he's perfect.' . . . I told [Williams] 'I'm basically doing a silent movie and I need to have the discipline of the way silent movie-music was written.' He understood completely and he was very excited about it immediately. So, it's been a great collaboration over twenty-five years.[9]

The film's final music score accompanied 88 minutes of the movie's 120-minute running time, a percentage unheard of since Max Steiner's 1930s heyday. The film, retroactively titled *Star Wars: Episode IV – A New Hope*, was an instant sensation that quickly eclipsed the previous box-office record-holder, Spielberg's *Jaws*, also scored by John Williams. By July, Williams' double-LP score had sold 650,000 copies, and would eventually sell 4 million, becoming the best-selling symphonic album of all time while earning Gold and Platinum certifications, an Oscar, and two Grammys.

THE COMPUTER REVOLUTION

It is hard to overstate the impact of the digital revolution on film and music, which began in the early 1990s. Until 1989, movies were shot on film stock, which was developed and physically cut on flatbed editors using razor blades, and then spliced together with tape. This process of film editing is called *linear* or *destructive editing* because the editor works their way through the film in sequence, shot by shot, and makes physical cuts to the film stock.

By the year 2000, nearly all films were being shot on digital cameras and edited using computer software. Editing on the computer is called *non-linear* or *non-destructive*, because the editor can scroll to any scene in the film and join or rejoin shots in any order as many times as needed.

A similar revolution took place in the world of music. Analog recording, which had defined the music industry from its inception, is the recording of music directly to tape. Just like in filmmaking, music was previously recorded onto analog tape in a professional recording studio and physically edited by sound engineers who cut the tape and spliced pieces together. The recordings consisted of either the composer performing the instruments themselves or musicians hired to play instruments for the recording. By 2000, composers could make recordings at home on their personal computers using specialized software like Pro Tools, Logic, and Cubase. They also began utilizing software and sound libraries that can reproduce the sounds of any instrument, including an entire orchestra, accurately. This allows composers to listen to their music exactly how it will sound in the film prior to the orchestra recording.

Before digital technology, the first time the director and composer heard the music in its final form was at the recording session, which also meant that any changes the director wanted needed to be done during the recording session. With this digital breakthrough, the director could now hear the music as it was being written and request edits, making the new process dramatically less expensive and time-consuming.

This shift to composing music using software removed the requirement that film composers possess a classical music background and formal education. Prior to the advent of digital technology, the only way for a composer to communicate their musical ideas was through written sheet music, which was performed and recorded by live musicians. With the advent of computer-assisted playback, composers could now compose on their computers and hear their music immediately. This new approach allowed popular musicians and producers the opportunity to score for film, which explains why the 1990s saw the rise of music producer-turned-film composers like Danny Elfman (Oingo Boingo), Mark Mothersbaugh (DEVO), Trevor Rabin (YES), James Newton Howard (Elton John Band), and, most consequentially, Hans Zimmer.

HANS ZIMMER

Hans Zimmer is the most influential composer in film-music history since Max Steiner. Both composers stood at a moment of great technological innovation, and both mastered the use of that technology to change the way film music was written and produced. Whereas Steiner created the first film-score template using traditional romantic orchestral music and thematic development (leitmotif), Zimmer expanded Steiner's template to include a much broader musical palate, which could include everything from rock guitar, experimental music, and synthesizer, to sound design and traditional orchestral scoring.

In the words of film-music theorist and composer Dan Golding:

> It's like a rock band playing through an orchestra. . . . For someone like Zimmer, you perform every note, which is then massaged by all of these people. You've got sound designers, synth designers, people who are there just to program these digital instruments. The end result is music that is created for a computer to play.[10]

Experimentation is at the heart of Zimmer's approach, resulting in the creation of a unique sound world for each score. As Zimmer himself explains, designing and creating sounds in the computer is a large part of his creative process:

> A computer is a musical instrument that needs just as much practice as when you practice piano or the violin or the cello, or whatever. You have to become fairly virtuosic at programming.[11]

First working as a musician and producer for New Wave bands in the 1980s – notably programming synthesizer on The Buggles' 1980 hit "Video Killed the

Radio Star" – Zimmer brought the studio-recording technique of his early days into the vocabulary of modern film music. The sound of the recording was suddenly of equal importance to the musical material being recorded, becoming a parameter in itself to express emotion. Zimmer was the first to create an orchestral sample library, which comprises recordings of orchestral instruments that can be played with a MIDI keyboard and computer software. This sampled orchestra gives him the opportunity to hear the orchestra and work with orchestral sounds before having the expensive and tedious final recording session, as well as play these "computer orchestra mockups" for the director and get feedback.

Whereas George Lucas never heard any of the *Star Wars* score until the orchestra recording session, with the sample orchestra in the computer, Hans Zimmer can recreate the sound of the orchestral recording in his studio while composing and share it with the director all along the way. Composing therefore becomes an even more intimate collaboration with the filmmaker. Director Christopher Nolan – who has worked with Zimmer on six films, including *Inception* (2010), *Interstellar* (2014), *Dunkirk* (2017), and *The Dark Knight* trilogy – says:

> Hans is one of the great masters of finding the sound of things: not just what the tunes are, not just what the notes are, but how they're played, what the voices are of the thing.[12]

Given the sonic possibilities that the computer opened up, each film can become a unique musical landscape. It's not uncommon for new sounds or instruments to be created for a particular score. For the film *Dune* (2021), Hans Zimmer commissioned the woodwind player Pedro Eustache to build a 21-foot contrabass duduk, a supersized version of the ancient Armenian woodwind instrument, out of PVC pipe, while having artist Chas Smith create metallic sculptures from springs, saw blades, and SpaceX engines that could be struck, scraped, and bowed. These sounds were then processed through computer software to create the fantastical, never-heard-before sound world of the *Dune* score. Of his process, Zimmer continues:

> The first thing I need to do is figure out an idea, something I haven't done before, because otherwise I get a bit bored. So there has to be a concept. And then the concept usually is something . . . impossible to do. I spend as much time experimenting . . . making up sounds. I spend far too much time playing with synthesizers and making sounds for the project until finally somebody says, 'You know, we're running out of time, we've got to get this movie done.'[13]

It's important to note that Zimmer approaches film composition not as a solo artist, but as a collective and highly collaborative endeavor. He employs a team of assistants ranging from instrumental musicians, sound designers, synth programmers, recording engineers, orchestrators, and additional composers who he works with to create each score.

OUTSIDE THE BOX

Hans Zimmer's experimental approach to the creation of film music has not only affected how film composers work and think about the film score. It has also had a significant impact on the musical choices of directors. In recent years, filmmakers working inside and outside of mainstream cinema have grown increasingly interested in experimenting with more unpredictable and unorthodox sounds in their film scores.

The new generation of independent directors has searched for a musical aesthetic beyond traditional film scoring as they enter the industry. Since the budget for indie films is usually tight, the directors have no other option but to make the most out of limited available music resources, which often means collaborating closely with musicians, bands, and producers to create something unique and unheard.

Jonny Greenwood, Mica Levi, Jóhan Jóhannsson, and the team of Trent Reznor and Atticus Ross are just a few names that have moved the needle in the film industry with their unconventional and individualistic film scores. By deconstructing the historical film-scoring traditions and opting for experimental sounds and techniques, these composers have established new trends in film music.

JONNY GREENWOOD

Jonny Greenwood has spent the majority of his nearly 30-year career as a musician behind one of the biggest rock bands in the world, Radiohead, and is responsible for shaping their distinctive sound and compositional style. Greenwood ventured into film scoring in 2003 when he composed the music for the documentary *Bodysong*. He has gone on to write notable scores to films such as *There Will Be Blood* (2007), *The Master* (2012), *Phantom Thread* (2018), and *The Power of the Dog* (2021).

In his scores, Greenwood creates a very unique blend of modernist compositional techniques and pop music production. He is known for his use of clusters, aleatoric techniques, and extended techniques, as well as his focus on sonic materiality and texture. Greenwood comments on the collaborative process and technology:

> It's sort of similar, I suppose, and it's lots of the same technology and lots of techniques from working with Radiohead. Is it the same? Yeah, I mean, I always compare it to being in a band with the director and editor and the people who are making a film. I quite enjoy that, suddenly getting to a group of people and feeling like you're in a band with them and are working for the same cause.[14]

TRENT REZNOR AND ATTICUS ROSS

Trent Reznor has led two wildly successful musical careers: one as the leader of the industrial-rock phenomenon Nine Inch Nails and the other as a film composer, in collaboration with Atticus Ross, with whom he has composed several film scores, beginning with their Oscar-winning score for *The Social Network* (2010), and followed by, among others, *The Girl with the Dragon Tattoo* (2011), *Gone Girl* (2014), *Mid90s* (2018), *Bird Box* (2018), HBO's *Watchmen* (2019), *Mank* (2020), and Pixar's *Soul* (2020), for which they won a second Oscar.

Masterfully combining the worlds of industrial rock and electronics, their collaborations often feature sparse, minimalistic arrangements that rely heavily on electronic sounds, synthesizers, and ambient textures, which can range from the tension and edge of *The Girl with the Dragon Tattoo* to the playful and uplifting children's music for *Soul*, co-written with Jon Batiste. They frequently use unconventional instruments or sound sources to create unique and otherworldly soundscapes that can be both haunting and beautiful.

Reznor recounts their first film-scoring process:

> We both had goosebumps watching [*The Social Network*] and in particular that title scene where the track we call 'Hand Covers Bruise' plays. When we wrote that I don't think we were both thinking, here's the main title theme, you know, but seeing it in there . . . I was amazed at how much the music could change your expectation of the film and your impression and set the whole tone. Not that I didn't know music could do that, but seeing it do that, it was pretty eye opening and just an exciting experience to witness and be a part of.[15]

MICA LEVI

Mica Levi, better known as Micachu, is a classically trained composer, songwriter, singer, and producer who, for the best part of a decade, has been mixing up everything from pop, indie, punk, and electronica to prestigious orchestras. In 2014, Levi branched out into film composing by composing the score for the Jonathan Glazer film *Under the Skin* (2014), and the original score for Pablo Larran's *Jackie* (2016) was nominated for an Academy Award.

Levi's music often combines elements of classical, electronic, and pop music, resulting in a sound that is both complex and memorable. Her compositions are characterized by their intricate rhythms, unusual chord progressions, and distinctive melodies, which often feature unexpected intervals and harmonies. Levi's music is also notable for its use of unconventional instrumentation and sound sources. She frequently incorporates found sounds and field recordings into their compositions, creating a sense of texture and atmosphere that is both organic and otherworldly. Levi also uses unusual instruments, such as the viola da gamba, to create a unique sound that is distinctly her own. Remembering her introduction to film scoring, Levi says:

> Composing for a film was such new territory for me that I approached *Under The Skin* like it could suddenly be gone tomorrow. I actually kept it a secret from a lot of people while I was working on it. The first call came from out of the blue, and when I went to meet Jonathan Glazer and [music producer] Peter Raeburn, they showed me some footage and we talked about what the music could be in a pretty abstract way. Jon didn't prescribe anything; he just asked me to follow my own trajectory.[16]

JÓHANN JÓHANNSSON

Jóhann Jóhannsson was an Icelandic composer, musician, and producer who was known for his innovative and atmospheric music. His musical style was characterized by its use of orchestral and electronic elements, often combining the two to create a sound that was both haunting and beautiful. He was known for his ability to create atmospheric soundscapes, using repeating patterns and drones to create a sense of tension and unease.

His film works include the original scores for the Denis Villeneuve films *Prisoners* (2013), *Sicario* (2015), and *Arrival* (2016), and for James Marsh's *The Theory of Everything* (2014), earning Oscar nominations for both *The Theory of Everything* and *Sicario*. On finding his way into film music, Jóhannsson said:

> It's really through my albums as a solo artist that, you know, filmmakers started to notice me. I worked in theater a lot in Iceland, where I got the chance to write a lot of music over a period of time, which was a great opportunity to develop my style and develop my sound. Once my records got out there, they started to get licensed for films and things like that. And then filmmakers started to approach me to write film scores. Kind of a very organic process in a way.[17]

CONCLUSION

In recent years, we've been hearing more and more experimental music in the movies. Dissonant traditional instruments can be combined with electronics. Bizarre soundscapes produced with complex modular synthesizers can create a fusion between organic sound sources and artificial sounds. What makes these eccentric experimental film scores so relevant in today's cinema is an unsettling sensation of the unknown, conveyed by the sounds we've never heard before, which allows film directors and score composers to unearth the storytelling capacity of obscure, unconventional music in horror, psychological dramas, thrillers, and other genres.

Simply put, the diversity of films and approaches to film music in this day and age is staggering. Never before has such a wide variety of music or types of musicians been as active in the medium of film music. As of the writing of this book in 2023, one can see a tremendous range of musical styles, from Ben Frost's experimental score to *1899* and *Dark*, to the vintage 1980s synths of Kyle Dixon and Michael Stein's score for *Stranger Things* (2016–). Kris Bowers is composing period music for *Bridgerton* (2020), which also contains Regency-era string quartet arrangements of songs from artists like Taylor Swift, Billie Elish, Pink and Maroon 5. At the same time, the Star Wars and Marvel franchises have faithfully maintained the Golden Age film-scoring style of Max Steiner with some added contemporary synth flavors for modern taste.

CHAPTER SUMMARY

- The evolution of film music is guided by technological advances in audio in film.
- Silent films relied on live musicians because there was no technology to synchronize sound to the moving image.
- The invention of the Vitaphone in 1925 allowed for sound to be synchronized to film, with *The Jazz Singer* ushering in a new era of "talkies."
- Max Steiner's score for *King Kong* was one of the very first original orchestral film scores, setting the template for how films were scored.

- In 1977, John Williams single-handedly revived the sound of the big Golden Age Hollywood orchestra with his score to *Star Wars*.
- Hans Zimmer redefined the process of film scoring with his use of computer, synthesizers, and samplers, allowing directors to hear the in-progress score before the orchestra recording session.
- Experimental composers like Jonny Greenwood, Mica Levi, Jóhan Jóhannsson, and Trent Reznor and Atticus Ross are applying new techniques and backgrounds to create never-before-heard sounds.

NOTES

1 American Film Institute (2016, August 9). *Steven Spielberg Praises John Williams*.https://www.youtube.com/watch?v=tJY5l6I253c

2 Hans Zimmer Teaches Film Scoring. www.masterclass.com/classes/hans-zimmer-teaches-film-scoring

3 Spraggins, Mark (2022). *Film-Music-Org, History & Survey of Film Music*. http://www.film-music.org/max-steiner-and-king-kong.html

4 Schreibman, Myrl A. and Max Steiner (2004). "On Gone With the Wind, Selznick, and the Art of 'Mickey Mousing': An Interview With Max Steiner". *Journal of Film and Video*, 56(1): 41–50. http://www.jstor.org/stable/20688442

5 Judd, Timothy (2015, December 30). "Thoughts on John Williams' New Star Wars Score". *The Listeners Club*. https://thelistenersclub.com/2015/12/30/thoughts-on-john-williams-new-star-wars-score/

6 Thompson, Simon (2020, January 30) "How George Lucas' Ideas Blazed Trails for Dolby Sound Over 40 Years of 'Star Wars'". *Variety*. https://variety.com/2020/artisans/awards/george-lucas-dolby-sound-star-wars-1203487459/

7 Ray Dolby: Inventing the Future of Entertainment. https://www.dolby.com/about/leadership/ray-dolby/#gref

8 Eicke, Stephan "Of Vaders and Raiders, Interview With Ben Burtt on Film Music and Sound Design". *Media Sound Hamburg*. https://mediasoundhamburg.de/en/of-vaders-and-raiders/

9 Burlingame, Jon (2012, February 8). "Spielberg and Lucas on Williams". *The Film Music Society*. http://www.filmmusicsociety.org/news_events/features/2012/020812.html

10 Dan Golding (2016, September 15). "A Theory of Film Music". *YouTube*. https://www.youtube.com/watch?v=UcXsH88XlKM

11 Mix With the Masters (2021, August 27). "Hans Zimmer's Use of Computers and Samples in Orchestral Music". *YouTube*. https://www.youtube.com/watch?v=_LHyNYRtwR8

12 Elegyscores (2011, March 30). "Hans Zimmer – Making of Inception Soundtrack". *YouTube*. https://www.youtube.com/watch?v=W1FIv7rFbv4

13 Mix With the Masters (2020, July 18). "Writing to Picture With Hans Zimmer". *YouTube*. https://www.youtube.com/watch?v=sj2PdzPzyYY

14 Unofficial Radiohead Interview (2022, March 11). "Soundtracking w/Edith Bowman – Interview–Jonny Greenwood". *YouTube*.https://www.youtube.com/watch?v=Fll8OSjXrYs

15 Jack Cole (2021, March 23). "The Social Network: Trent Reznor, Atticus Ross, and David Fincher on the Score". *YouTube*. https://www.youtube.com/watch?v=8oLsch7q3pc

16 Melt Yourself Down (2020, April 12). "100% Isolated: Pete and Mica Levi". *YouTube*. https://www.youtube.com/watch?v=XwRM4XHcIws

17 "Making Music of Sicario – Johann Johannsson". *YouTube*. (no video available).

2

FILM MUSIC FROM AROUND THE WORLD

FRENCH FILM MUSIC

As measured by the number of films produced annually, France has long had the most successful film industry in Europe, and it continues to have a particularly strong film industry, in part due to government protections. Many historians consider Paris to be the official birthplace of cinema. In 1895, the Lumière brothers introduced the *cinematographe*, the first motion picture system, and Paris has the highest density of cinemas in the world, with the nation as a whole boasting one cinema screen per every 31 French residents.

The earliest French film composers were primarily classical musicians who were brought in to create music for silent films. As covered in the previous chapter, one of the first notable French film composers was Camille Saint-Saëns, who composed the music for the first French feature-length film, *L'Assassinat du duc de Guise* (or *The Assassination of the Duke of Guise*) in 1908.

During the 1930s, French cinema experienced its own golden age, when composers such as Georges Auric, Joseph Kosma, and Maurice Jaubert began to create more experimental and modern film scores. These composers were heavily influenced by jazz and popular music, and they began to incorporate these styles into their film music.

FRENCH NEW WAVE

The French New Wave (*La Nouvelle Vague* in French) was a film movement that emerged in the late 1950s. The filmmakers associated with the movement, such as Jean-Luc Godard, François Truffaut, and Éric Rohmer, were known for their rejection of traditional Hollywood conventions and their experimentation with new film techniques and storytelling styles. The French New Wave films were often shot on location with hand-held cameras, and featured a more improvisational, documentary-style approach to filmmaking.

DOI: 10.4324/9781003289722-2

Some examples of Hollywood directors influenced by the French New Wave include Martin Scorsese, Quentin Tarantino, and Brian De Palma, all of whom have been known to incorporate some of the visual and stylistic elements of the French New Wave into their own films.

The French New Wave filmmakers often used music in their films in a way that was unconventional for the time. One of the key ways in which they used music was through the use of *diegetic* music, which means that the music is heard by the characters within the film and is part of the story. They often used popular music and jazz in their soundtracks, as well as classical music, to create a sense of spontaneity and reflect the youth culture of the time. The scores often sound like they could be the music the characters are listening to in the film itself. The French New Wave directors also frequently use the technique of mismatching the music with the on-screen visuals, creating a sense of contrast, irony, or dissonance, a technique also called playing "against the picture." An excellent example of this is Jean Constantin's score to François Trauffaut's film *The 400 Blows*, in which Constantin's music remains upbeat regardless of the tragedy that befalls the main character, Antoine Doinel.

Explaining the role of music in the French New Wave, Jean-Luc Godard said:

> The stylistic aesthetic which characterizes the New Wave of French cinema is a return to a natural realism and a self-conscious use of Hollywood cinematic cliché. This can be seen in the score to *Breathless*. There is relatively little music in the film and each individual cue feels more like a piece of diegetic source music than actual score that was created to enhance the emotion of the film. Oftentimes the visual images are accentuated by a self-conscious over-exaggeration of the musical style which could be a 'jazzy detective' music which only plays briefly to an over-the-top romantic string cue for two lovers speaking by a car. The brevity and exaggerated nature leads to a self-consciousness.

The French New Wave filmmakers often used a variety of different composers for their film soundtracks, including both classical musicians and popular song-writers. Two of the most notable composers associated with the movement are Georges Delerue and Michel Legrand.

Georges Delerue began his career composing for French New Wave films like Truffaut's *Jules and Jim* (1962), Godard's *Contempt* (1954), and Alain Resnais' *Hiroshima, mon amour* (1959), before continuing his career in Hollywood on over 350 scores, most notably Oliver Stone's *Platoon* (1984). His style ranges from songs, marches, stride piano, and intimate chamber music in Truffaut's films, to traditional Hollywood orchestral scores in *Platoon* and *Black Robe* (1991).

Michel Legrand composed the music for several French New Wave films, including Jacques Demy's *The Umbrellas of Cherbourg* (1964), *The Young Girls of Rochefort* (1967), and Agnès Varda's *Cléo from 5 to 7* (1961). In addition to earning Academy Awards for his scores to *Summer of '42* (1971) and *Yentl* (1983), he was also a prolific songwriter, winning an Oscar for his song "The Windmills of Your Mind" from the *Thomas Crown Affair* (1968). Legrand's approach to film music is song-oriented with its roots in the jazz styles of the 1960s and 1970s, as well as Broadway and the Great American Songbook.

Outside of the New Wave movement, at least two other very important French film composers found their way to Hollywood. Maurice Jarre composed the scores for popular Hollywood films such as *The Man Who Would Be King* (1975), *Fatal Attraction* (1987), *Dead Poets Society* (1989), and *Ghost* (1990), winning Best Original Score for *Lawrence of Arabia, Doctor Zhivago* (1965), and *A Passage to India* (1984). He is also the father of well-known electronic composer and producer Jean-Michel Jarre. Many of Jarre's best-known scores hark back to the Golden Age of Hollywood, with big, sweeping orchestral gestures with a distinctly European sensibility.

More recently, Paris-born composer Alexandre Desplat has won two Academy Awards for his scores to *The Grand Budapest Hotel* (2014) and *The Shape of Water* (2017), in addition to his work on *The Golden Compass* (2007), *The King's Speech* (2010), *Harry Potter and the Deathly Hallows* (2010–11), *Godzilla* (2014), and *The Secret Life of Pets* (2016). Desplat is also known for his ability to blend different musical styles and traditions in his work. For example, in his score for *The Grand Budapest Hotel*, he combined traditional European orchestral music with Eastern European folk music, while in *The Shape of Water*, he blended elements of classical, jazz, and electronic music to create a dreamy, atmospheric score.

ITALIAN FILM MUSIC

Italian cinema has influenced film movements worldwide since its inception.

Occurring in the late 1910s, Italian Futurism was the earliest European avant-garde cinema movement. After a period of decline in the 1920s, the Italian film industry was revitalized by the introduction of sound films in the 1930s. While the fascist government of Italy provided financial support for the nation's film industry, notably the construction of Cinecittà, the largest film studio in Europe, it also engaged in censorship, resulting in the production of numerous propaganda films in the late 1930s. Some of Italy's most notable directors include Federico Fellini, Roberto Rosellini, Bernardo Bertolucci, Sergio Leone, and Dario Argento.

FEDERICO FELLINI AND NINO ROTA

Federico Fellini was an Italian film director and screenwriter, considered one of the most influential and widely renowned filmmakers in the history of cinema. Directing over 20 feature films, many of which were highly acclaimed and awarded, he is best-known for his films *La Strada* (1954), *La Dolce Vita* (1960), *8½* (1963), and *Fellini Satyricon* (1969), which are all considered masterpieces of Italian cinema.

Fellini's films were known for their imaginative, surreal, and often dream-like storytelling, and for their use of symbolism and metaphor. He was also known for his use of non-professional actors and his creative collaboration with his cast and crew.

One of Fellini's most notable and recurrent collaborators was Nino Rota, an Italian composer who worked with Fellini on almost all of his films, from the 1950s until Rota's death in 1979. Rota's music for Fellini's films was often characterized by its lush, romantic melodies and its incorporation of elements of Italian folk music and opera. The music was a key component of Fellini's films, and helped to create the hypnagogic atmosphere they are known for.

Rota's style is recognized by its use of melody, traditional harmonic structures, and a strong influence from classical music and jazz. Though he composed for a few Hollywood films, his style was ultimately European, in contrast to the sweeping, epic aesthetic of Max Steiner. Meanwhile, his most popular scores were for an Italian-American director, Francis Ford Coppola, for whom he scored both *The Godfather* (1972) and *The Godfather Part II* (1974).

According to Fellini:

> The most precious collaborator I have ever had, I say it straight away and don't even have to hesitate, was Nino Rota. Between us, immediately, a complete, total harmony. . . . He had a geometric imagination, a musical approach worthy of celestial spheres. He thus had no need to see images from my movies. When I asked him about the melodies he had in mind to comment one sequence or another, I clearly realized he was not concerned with images at all. His world was inner, inside himself, and reality had no way to enter it.[1]

SERGIO LEONE AND ENNIO MORRICONE

From the mid-1950s to the end of the 1970s, Italian cinema reached a position of great prestige, both nationally and abroad. The best known of these films are the *Spaghetti Westerns*, an Italian spin on the American "cowboy and Indian" stories, which achieved huge popularity in the mid-1960s.

The master of this genre, Sergio Leone wrote and directed some of the most iconic and influential Westerns in the history of cinema, including the Dollars Trilogy consisting of *A Fistful of Dollars* (1964), *For a Few Dollars More* (1965), and *The Good, the Bad and the Ugly* (1966) – which launched the career of Clint Eastwood – as well as the epic *Once Upon a Time in the West* (1968).

Leone's films were known for their epic storytelling, larger-than-life characters, and striking imagery. Leone's Westerns were not just a mere representation of their American counterparts, but a reinterpretation of them from a European perspective. He brought a new visual style to the previously low-brow genre, using long shots, close-ups, masterful image composition, and a new way of telling the story, with melodramatic editing and a focus on the characters' inner thoughts and emotions.

Equally associated with Leone's iconic films, if not more so, is composer Ennio Morricone. Often characterized by its use of unconventional instrumentation, such as whistling, electric guitars, and the human voice, Morricone also used unorthodox techniques such as silence and unusual harmonic progressions.

Morricone's score for *The Good, the Bad and the Ugly* has become one of the most recognizable and iconic pieces of film music in history. Prominently featuring trumpet, harmonica, and a choir, the score uses a mix of orchestral and electronic instruments to convey the massive drama of the film. Morricone's musical approach to the Spaghetti Westerns has become the template upon which many subsequent scores are based. His influence can be heard in modern Westerns such as *Unforgiven* (1992) and *3:10 to Yuma* (2007), as well as *Kill Bill: Volume 2* (2003) and *Pirates of the Caribbean: At World's End* (2007).

In the words of Sergio Leone:

> I've always felt that music is more expressive than dialogue. I've always said that my best dialogue and screenwriter is Ennio Morricone. Because, many times, it is more important a note or an orchestration than a line said.[2]

Morricone remains one of the world's most prolific film composers, with over 530 film scores to his name. Outside of his work with Sergio Leone, he won two Academy Awards and six BAFTA Awards, and is best known for his scores to *The Mission* (1986), *The Untouchables* (1987), *Bugsy* (1991), and *The Hateful Eight* (2016).

GIALLO AND THE BIRTH OF MODERN HORROR

Italian Giallo films, particularly those produced by directors such as Mario Bava and Dario Argento in the 1960s and 1970s, have had a significant influence on the horror films of today. The stylistic and narrative elements of Giallo, such as the use of graphic violence, eroticism, and an emphasis on mystery, alienation, and paranoia, have influenced many Hollywood films, including *Halloween*, *The Silence of the Lambs* (1991), *Basic Instinct* (1992), and *Kill Bill: Volume 1* (2003), with filmmakers like Quentin Tarantino and Brian De Palma making direct reference to this lush style of horror.

With their inventive use of electronic instruments and dissonant chords, Giallo-style scoring has also been a major influence on the sound design and scoring of modern horror. Two of the most important Giallo composers were Ennio Morriconne and Bruno Nicoli, who composed orchestrally based scores with the addition of electronic elements. Some Giallo directors experimented with the use of rock music and electronically driven scores, with Dario Argento most famously working with Italian rock band Goblin on several of his films, most notably *Susperia* (1977). Following in the footsteps of Giallo was Mike Oldfield's famous "Tubular Bells" track in *The Exorcist* (1973) and the synth scores of John Carpenter, which eventually evolved into Charlie Clouser's electronic and industrial-rock-driven scores in the *Saw* series.

JAPANESE FILM MUSIC

Japanese film music has a rich history influenced by various traditional and modern musical styles. One of the most well-known traditional styles is Kabuki, which is a form of theater that features music, dance, and drama. Kabuki often features the shamisen, a three-stringed instrument that is plucked with a plectrum, and the music is characterized by its use of rhythms, melodies, and instrumentation that evoke historic Japan.

During the Silent Era, Japanese cinema saw the rise of the *jidaigeki*, a genre of film that depicts the lives of samurai and other historical figures, and the *bunraku*, a genre that tells stories of everyday life. These films were often shot on location and used non-professional actors. The advent of sound in the 1930s brought a new level of realism to Japanese cinema and allowed for a wider range of stories to be told.

After World War II, Japanese cinema entered its golden age, which lasted from the late 1940s to the early 1960s. This period saw the rise of the "big four" directors: Akira Kurosawa, Yasujirō Ozu, Kenji Mizoguchi, and Mikio Naruse. These directors, along with many others, created films that were both critically acclaimed and popular with audiences.

YASUJIRŌ OZU AND TAKANOBU SAITŌ

Yasujirō Ozu is considered one of the most important directors in Japanese cinema. Ozu's films often depict the everyday lives of middle-class families in Japan, and many of his films explore themes of tradition, family, and change. His most widely beloved films include *Late Spring* (1949), *Tokyo Story* (1953), and *An Autumn Afternoon* (1962). In a 2012 Sight & Sound poll, *Tokyo Story* was voted the third-greatest film of all time by critics worldwide, with 358 directors and filmmakers in the same poll picking it as the greatest film ever made.

Long takes, static camera shots, and minimal camera movement define Ozu's style. Instead of fades or dissolves, he utilized pillow shots – static shots of landscapes, objects, or other details that are not directly related to the story, but instead serve as an artistic interlude. They can be used to establish a mood or atmosphere, to provide a transition between scenes, or to add visual interest to the film. Pillow shots are often quite beautiful and evocative, and can be seen as a form of cinematic poetry. During these shots he would employ music, which would begin at the conclusion of one scene, continue through the static transition, and fade into the next scene. Most of the music used in Ozu's films occur in these transitions and there is very little music used during the scenes.

Some excellent examples can be found in Takanobu Saitô's score to Ozu's *Tokyo Story* where, after a scoreless scene of dialogue, the music begins as we see shots of factories and modern railway stations contrasting with simple shots of day-to-day life, such as a woman sweeping a home. Saitô's music provides a touch of nostalgia with a gentle orchestral score clearly influenced by the Hollywood tradition and does not make use of traditional Japanese instruments or compositions. Saitô would go on to compose music to Ozu's *Equinox Flower* (1958), and *Late Autumn* (1960).

AKIRA KUROSAWA

Akira Kurosawa was one of the most influential filmmakers in the history of cinema. He directed over 30 films, many of which are considered masterpieces of Japanese cinema, which include *Rashomon* (1950), *Seven Samurai* (1954), *Yojimbo* (1961), and *Ran* (1985).

Kurosawa's films were often set in feudal Japan, but they dealt with universal themes such as the human condition, the nature of good and evil, and the search for meaning in life. His films were often highly critical of the traditional values and social structures of Japanese society, and they often depicted the struggles of ordinary people.

Kurosawa's early films often featured music composed by Fumio Hayasaka, who incorporated traditional Japanese instruments such as the shamisen and koto into his scores. Hayasaka's music was known for its use of dissonance and unconventional harmonies, which helped to create a sense of unease and tension in the films. This blend of Japanese traditional instruments and melodies with the Western orchestra gave Hayasaka a distinctive and original voice in film music. Hayasaka's score to *Roshamon* is a very interesting blend of Hollywood-style scoring, where the music is tightly synchronized with the action of the film, using traditional Japanese instruments.

Reflecting on their creative partnership, Kurosowa said:

> I changed my thinking about musical accompaniment from the time Hayasaka Fumio began working with me as composer of my film scores. Up until that time film music was nothing more than accompaniment – for a sad scene there was always sad music. This is the way most people use the music, and it is ineffective. But from *Drunken Angel* onward, I have used light music for some key sad scenes, and my way of using music has differed from the norm. I don't put it in where most people do. Working with Hayasaka, I began to think in terms of the counterpoint of sound and image as opposed to the union of sound and image.[3]

After Hayasaka's death in 1955, Kurosawa began collaborating with Tôru Takemitsu, the most successful Japanese composer of the 20th century and argu-ably the most well-known Asian composer after World War II. Beginning his film career as Hayasaka's assistant, Takemitsu composed music for concert halls, films, televisions, and commercials before becoming best-known outside of Japan for his more than 130 "serious" concert works. However, he was also a prolific film composer who wrote over 100 soundtracks to his name.

Takemitsu composed the music for two of Kurosawa's later films, *Dodes'ka-den* (1970) and *Ran*. Takemitsu's music was known for its incorporation of Western clas-sical music and avant-garde techniques, and his use of electronic instruments and sound effects. His diverse scores often featured a mix of orchestral and electronic elements, and they were able to convey a wide range of emotions and atmosphere.

While working on *Ran*, Takemitsu was interested in composing a score solely of traditional Japanese vocal and instrumental styles, while Kurosawa, who was not nicknamed "The Emperor" for nothing, insisted on a Mahler-influenced orchestral score in the Western classical style. In spite of Takemitsu's resistance to the director's wishes, the resulting score is remembered as one of his best.

GODZILLA

Ishiro Honda was a Japanese film director best known for directing the original *Godzilla*, as well as many other *kaiju* (or *strange beast*) films, war films, and science fiction films. Beginning his career as an assistant director to Yasujirō Ozu, Honda directed many films, but he is mostassociated with the Godzilla franchise, which is the longest-running film series in history. In addition to the first *Godzilla* (1954), Honda directed the subsequent *King Kong vs. Godzilla* (1962), *Mothra vs. Godzilla* (1964), and *Godzilla vs. Megalon* (1973), as well as other kaiju classics like *Rodan* (1956), *Mothra* (1961), *Ghidorah* (1964), and *Destroy All Monsters* (1968).

A composer and ethnomusicologist who scored over 280 films, Akira Ifukube scored many of Honda's movies. He is best known for the iconic "Godzilla March" theme, which has been used in many of the later films in the series. The theme, which features a mix of orchestral and percussion elements, is often associated with the monster and is considered one of the most recognizable pieces of film music in history. Ifukube's style is very influenced by Max Steiner's *King Kong* score and the music of Bernard Herrmann, which is one of the reasons why his music has been embraced in Hollywood.

RUSSIAN FILM MUSIC

Russians fell in love with the art of cinema from early on. The first Russian dramatized film was produced in 1908, making Russian cinema one of the oldest. By 1913, Russia had over 1,300 cinemas and had produced over 100 films, exerting a significant influence on its European and American counterparts.

As the Russian Revolution progressed in the early 20th century, a large number of directors emigrated, leaving the Russian film industry in disarray. In 1919, the film industry was nationalized, and shortly thereafter Moscow's VGIK was established as the world's first film school.

Under the Soviet government led by Vladimir Lenin, who once said, "Of all the arts, for us the cinema is the most important," filmmakers were granted creative freedom, paving the way for some of the most influential film theorists to date. Despite the relative freedom to experiment, it was made clear that films should be made for and about the average person, with the Marxist philosophy that the artist should view himself as an engineer or average worker rather than an artist. The filmmakers of this movement, who were heavily influenced by the theories of Russian formalist critics, sought to create a new film language that would reflect the revolutionary ideals of the Soviet state, using techniques such as montage, fragmentation, and symbolism to create films that were both political and artistic.

EISENSTEIN AND PROKOFIEV

Sergei Eisenstein was the most influential of the new generation of Soviet filmmakers who created an entirely new science of filmmaking based on Marxist dialectics, going far beyond the notion of moving pictures. The 1938 historical drama *Alexander Nevsky*, the first of Eisenstein's dramatic films to use sound, features a musical score by Sergei Prokofiev, the well-known classical composer of *Peter and the Wolf*, the ballet *Romeo and Juliet*, and seven symphonies. The film was a true collaboration, with portions of the film shot to Prokofiev's music and portions of Prokofiev's music composed to Eisenstein's footage, with Prokofiev viewing the rough cut as the initial step in composing its unique score. Eisenstein and Prokofiev's strong and technically innovative collaboration in the editing process produced a match of music and imagery that remains a standard for filmmakers, while the film's score remains arresting and memorable to this day.

Recalling his process with Prokofiev, Eisenstein said:

The projection-room is darkened . . . The picture runs on the screen . . .

And on the arm of the chair, nervously drumming, exactly like a Morse telegrapher, tap the relentlessly precise, long fingers of Prokofiev. Is Prokofiev beating time? No. He is 'beating' something more than that. He is detecting the structural laws governing the lengths and tempo in the edited pieces, harmonizing these with the actions and intonations of the characters. On the following day, he will send me the music which will permeate my montage structure, the structural laws of which he will carry into the rhythmic figure that his fingers tapped out.[4]

SHOSTAKOVICH

Taking over after Lenin, Joseph Stalin had a great interest in film, which he saw as a powerful tool for propaganda, believing that they should reflect the values of the Communist party while teaching its history and promoting the Soviet way of life.

Dmitry Shostakovich is one of the most celebrated Russian concert composers of the 20th century, known for his 15 symphonies, numerous chamber works, and concerti, many of which were composed under the pressure of government-imposed Soviet art standards.

Shostakovich's early works were well-received by Stalin and the Soviet government, and he was celebrated as a model for socialist realism in music. However, in 1936, Stalin attended a performance of Shostakovich's opera *Lady Macbeth of the Mtsensk District* and was reportedly displeased with its modernist elements. Following this, Shostakovich came under attack in the Soviet press, and his music was criticized for being "formalist" and "anti-Soviet." Despite this, Stalin was a great admirer of his film music and took a personal interest in seeing Shostakovich channeling his compositional ability into film.

Explaining the Soviet leader's influence on both Russian cinema and his own career within it, Shostakovich said:

Stalin was in charge of the film industry personally. . . . My own firm conviction is that film is an industry and not an art, but my participation in this industry of national importance saved me. More than once or twice. Stalin wanted our film industry to put out only masterpieces. He was convinced that under his brilliant leadership and personal guidance, it would do so. . . . He had his own confused notions about who could do what, and he decided that Shostakovich could write film scores. And he never changed his mind. Considering the situation, it would have been irrational for me to refuse to do film work.[5]

As time went on, Shostakovich's non-film music continued to be heavily censored by the Soviet government, and he came under pressure to conform to their expectations. Ultimately, he was forced to publicly denounce his own work, and suffered greatly under Stalin's regime.

The film music of both Prokofiev and Shostakovich is written in a similar style to their classical concert music. Many of their film scores became well-known concert pieces such as Prokofiev's "Alexander Nevsky Suite" and Shostakovich's "The Gadfly Suite." It is interesting to note that the musical vocabulary of their work is quite different from the classic Hollywood model, a consequence of Stalin's restriction on the number of Hollywood films allowed to be shown, which were seen as a symbol of the evils of capitalism, and because the Soviet composers were expected to create film music based on their own Russian traditions, both folk and classical.

TARKOVSKY

Andrei Tarkovsky was a Russian film director, writer, and film theorist, considered one of the greatest film directors of the 20th century. His films are known for their deeply philosophical and spiritual themes, and for their use of long takes, poetic imagery, and unconventional narrative structures. Tarkovsky's films often use music as an integral part of the storytelling and atmosphere, with the director very interested in the organization of sound and the intersection between sound design and music.

The music in Tarkovsky's films *Solaris* (1972), *The Mirror* (1975), and *Stalker* (1979) were composed by Eduard Artemyev, who was one of the most prominent Soviet composers of the time. He wrote his first composition in 1967, on one of the original synthesizers developed by the Soviet engineer Yevgeny Murzin, making him one of the very first composers of electronic music.

His score for Tarkovsky's *Solaris* is known for its innovative use of electronic instruments and sound effects. One of the most distinctive instruments used in the score is the theremin, an electronic instrument that produces a distinctive, ethereal sound that is often described as sounding like a human voice or a musical saw. Artemyev used the theremin to create the film's main theme, a haunting melody that is heard throughout the score. Artemyev also utilized a synthesizer, an electronic keyboard, and various sound generators, as well as a variety of unconventional sound effects and textures, such as the sounds of water droplets and buzzing insects.

Artemyev remembered his creative dynamic with Tarkovsky like this:

> [Tarkovsky] told me right away that he didn't need a composer at all, he needed the composer's ear and his masterful command of sound in order to mix music, to make sound effects, possibly to add some orchestra . . . so that the background sound is organized compositionally. He did not need music as a developing theme. 'This is not a concert,' he said. 'This is something special.'[6]

INDIAN FILM MUSIC

India is the largest maker of films in the world, producing a total of 2,446 feature films in 2019 alone, and the second oldest film industry in the world. In addition to making the most films of any nation, India also has the largest number of theater admissions and leads the globe in ticket sales, while coming in third in terms of revenue due to having some of the lowest ticket prices in the world.

Based in Mumbai (formerly Bombay), Bollywood is just one subset of the multi-lingual Indian film industry. Bollywood produces movies in Hindi, which is only one of the 22 local languages officially recognized by India's constitution. More or less, every one of the local languages has its own film sub-industries, with Tamil and Telugu being the biggest ones behind Bollywood.

The Indian music industry is dominated by Bollywood soundtracks, which account for nearly 80 percent of the country's music revenue. Over the course of more than half a century, these songs were the backbone of South Asian popular music and, along with Hindi films, an important cultural export to most countries in Asia and wherever the Indian diaspora reached.

To understand the role of Indian film music, you need to consider that, before the 1990s, there was virtually no such thing as non-film commercial music, except for traditional folk artists, although even this was rare. The recording industry came about when vinyl became widely available and served as a secondary market for film music, which was still written as a part of the movie and not as a standalone product.

An average Indian movie will feature between four and six original songs that fit into the narrative of the film. If the US produces around 600 movies per year, India's output is closer to 2,000, which means that around 10,000 original songs are produced each year to fulfill the needs of the film industry.

The approach to film music in India is very different from the conventional movie sync licensing in the West. Here's how the process works: the director and screenwriters will define the song's place in the script and therefore determine the narrative behind it. Then a music director and a lyricist (or *literati*) will write and compose an original piece of music that fits the setting and the storyline. Next, a professional playback singer will go into the studio to record a song for actors to lip-synch in the movie. That's how film music was produced in the 1930s, and not much has changed since then.

The history of Indian film music can be traced back to the early days of Indian cinema, with the first Indian motion picture, *Raja Harishchandra* (1913), which featured a simple background score. In the 1920s and 1930s, Indian film music began to develop its own unique style and identity, with the emergence of Indian film stars and the production of films in multiple languages.

During this period, Indian film music was heavily influenced by Indian classical and folk music, which was reflected in the compositions and arrangements used in films. The use of harmonium, sitar, and tabla became common, and the songs were often performed by trained classical singers. The lyrics of these songs were also deeply rooted in Indian culture and traditions.

In the 1940s and 1950s, Indian film music reached new heights of commercial and artistic success with the emergence of legendary music directors such as Naushad and S. D. Burman. They introduced Western orchestral elements and arrangements in Indian film music, which gave it a new dimension.

In the 1960s and 1970s, Indian film music continued to evolve and diversify, with the emergence of new music directors such as R. D. Burman, Laxmikant-Pyarelal, and Kalyanji-Anandji, who introduced new sounds and styles. This period also saw the rise of playback singing, where the songs were pre-recorded and lip-synced by actors.

Besides the mainstream commercial movies, India also offers a different approach to cinema. Originating in West Bengal around the 1950s, *Parallel Cinema* is a blanket term designated to a certain type of film that strays away from the conventions of popular mainstream cinema. Inspired by Italian Neorealism, Parallel Cinema began just before the French New Wave and Japanese New Wave, and was a precursor to the Indian New Wave of the 1960s.

In recent years, Indian film – and, by extension, Indian film music – has seen a resurgence in popularity, both domestically and internationally. Indian film music continues to evolve and diversify, with a wide range of languages and styles reflecting the diversity of Indian society and culture.

A. R. RAHMAN

A. R. Rahman is a highly acclaimed Indian film composer, record producer, and singer, widely considered one of the greatest film composers in the Indian film industry. He began his career in the early 1990s and has since composed music for over 150 films in various languages, including Hindi, Tamil, and Telugu.

One of Rahman's signature techniques is to incorporate traditional Indian instruments into his compositions such as the tabla, sitar, and veena, while also using electronic instruments and production techniques. This fusion of traditional and modern elements creates a unique and innovative sound that is instantly recognizable. Characterized by its infectious energy, catchy melodies, and eclectic mix of musical styles, Rahman's score for *Slumdog Millionaire* (2008) won the Oscar for Best Original Score, in addition to winning Best Original Song for the track "Jai Ho," which became a massive hit after the release of the film.

S. D. BURMAN AND R. D. BURMAN

Sachin Dev Burman was an Indian music composer and singer who was active in the Indian film industry from the 1930s to the 1970s. He composed music for over 150 films and is considered one of the most prominent music directors in the history of Indian cinema. Burman began his career as a music composer in the 1930s and quickly established himself as a prominent figure in the film industry, composing music for some of the most successful Indian films of his time, such as *Devdas* (1955), *Pather Panchali* (1955), and *Bandini* (1963).

Known for his ability to capture the spirit of the film and its subject, and for his ability to evoke strong emotional responses from audiences with catchy and memorable melodies, Burman was one of the first figures to blend Indian classical and folk music with Western elements, and for his use of unconventional instruments in his compositions. His music was heavily influenced by Indian classical music, and his use of harmonium, sitar, and able became common in film music as a result, as was his use of choral singing and innovative arrangements.

Following in his father's footsteps, S. D. Burman's only son, R. D. Burman, not only went on to carve out his own career, but, in many ways, he eclipsed his father's legacy. Scoring 331 films between the 1960s and 1990s, including songs that are still popular to this day, he remains one of the most successful and beloved music directors in Indian film history.

CHINESE FILM MUSIC

Paralleling the country's overall economic expansion, the Chinese movie industry has grown into a global force over the past several decades. Since 2010, it has had the third-largest film industry by number of feature films produced annually. For the past few years, the US and China have been in a neck-and-neck race for the largest global box office, with China becoming the first country to overtake North American box-office revenues in 2020. Building new movie theaters at a rapid clip – the country added nearly 6,700 new screens in 2021 alone – it expects to surpass a national total of 100,000 within the next five years, compared to 40,000 in the US.

The story of Chinese cinema combines three distinct film industries: those of China, Hong Kong, and Taiwan. Filmmaking was introduced in China in 1896, with the first Chinese film, *Dingjun Mountain*, made in 1905.

With the film industry centered in Shanghai in the first decades, when it was heavily influenced by Hollywood, it wasn't until the 1920s and 1930s that Chinese film began to develop its own unique style and identity, blending elements of traditional Chinese culture with Western filmmaking techniques.

In the 1940s, the Chinese film industry experienced a resurgence, with the emergence of the "Third Generation" of Chinese filmmakers. These filmmakers, such as Fei Mu and Zhang Shichuan, were known for their realistic and socially conscious films, which often dealt with the plight of the Chinese people during a time of war and political turmoil.

Then, in 1949, the Chinese Communist Party came to power and the film industry underwent significant changes yet again, when the government established the China Film Group Corporation (CFGC) and began to heavily regulate and control what was made. During this period, Chinese films were heavily censored and often used as a tool for propaganda.

In the 1980s and 1990s, the Chinese film industry began to liberalize, and a new wave of filmmakers emerged. These filmmakers were known for their ability to blend traditional Chinese culture with Western filmmaking, and for their ability to create films that resonated with audiences both in China and internationally.

In recent years, the Chinese film industry has experienced significant growth, with the success of Chinese films both domestically and internationally. Home to the largest film studio in the world, Hengdian World Studios, Chinese cinema is now one of the fastest growing in the world, with a wide range of films being produced in various languages and styles.

China is a unique film market in that it also protects its domestic industry by only allowing 34 foreign movies to be screened a year, making it difficult for overseas studios to capitalize on growing demand from the country's emerging middle class. Chinese censors are very rigid, and the government imposes strict guidelines and regulations on foreign films shown in China and foreign film companies that operate there.

DANTE LAM AND ELLIOT LEUNG

Dante Lam is a Hong Kong film director and producer. Known for his work in the Hong Kong film industry, particularly in the action genre, he began his career as a director in the late 1990s, and has since directed and produced several critically acclaimed and commercially successful films.

Lam's film *The Battle at Lake Changjin* (2021) is the most expensive film ever produced in China, with a budget of $200 million. The film grossed $913 million at the worldwide box office, making it the highest-grossing Chinese film of all time and the highest-grossing non-English film in the world. Lam's *Operation Red Sea* (2018) and *The Battle at Lake Changjin II* (2022) are also among the top ten highest-grossing domestic films in China. All three of these films are scored by Elliot Leung.

Elliot Leung was born in Hong Kong and, while studying in the US, he had the opportunity to be mentored by Marty O'Donnell, who composed the music for the video game series *Halo*. The compositional style of Elliot Leung is very much in the vein of epic Hollywood action films, which combine orchestra, percussion, and electronics. There is little use of traditional Chinese instruments, with Leung favoring the big orchestra-electronic hybrid sound that has come to characterize most of the US action franchises. Leung is the first film composer from Hong Kong to break into Hollywood.

Aside from Leung's activity as a film composer, the video game company Tencent Games invited him to compose for *Honor of Kings*, the highest-grossing mobile game of all time.

TAN DUN

Tan Dun is a Chinese-American composer and conductor best known in the film world for his Academy Award-winning score for *Crouching Tiger, Hidden Dragon* (2000), in addition to scoring *Fallen* (1998), *Hero* (2002), and *The Night Banquet* (2006).

Tan Dun's score for *Crouching Tiger, Hidden Dragon* is a groundbreaking work that blends traditional Chinese music with Western orchestration and modern electronic techniques. Featuring a mix of traditional Chinese instruments, such as the erhu, pipa, and guzheng, with Western orchestral instruments like the cello and violin, the score helped to popularize Chinese music and culture around the world. It also incorporates electronic sounds and ambient textures, creating a unique blend of old and new.

One of the most memorable tracks from the score is "The Eternal Vow," which features a beautiful and emotional duet between the cello and erhu. Throughout the score, Tan Dun uses a variety of techniques to create a sense of drama and tension, including sudden changes in dynamics, unexpected pauses, and dramatic swells of sound. He also incorporates themes and motifs, similar in structure to Max Steiner, that recur throughout the film, helping to tie the music to the story and characters. It is widely regarded as one of the most influential and iconic film scores of the modern era and certainly one that brought Chinese musical culture to the forefront of film scoring.

CHAPTER SUMMARY

- Each culture of filmmaking brought with it a unique way to score.
- The French New Wave filmmakers used the score to feel "diegetic" and to play contrary to the emotions evoked by the images, in opposition to the Hollywood style.
- Italian film-scoring styles, especially Ennio Morricone's Spaghetti Western and Giallo thrillers, had a big influence on Hollywood from the 1970s onwards.
- Japanese films, especially those of Kurosowa, introduced the use of traditional Asian instruments to the vocabulary of Hollywood film.
- The classical composers Shostakovich and Prokofiev were central to the development of Russian film.
- Film music in India is dominated by soundtracks, with original songs being an essential part of Indian filmmaking.
- China is set to be the largest box office in the world, and the style of film scoring is very similar to the epic blockbusters of Hollywood.

NOTES

1 Judd, Timothy (2021, September 17). "Nino Rota's First Symphony: Sweeping Cinematic Grandeur". *The Listeners Club.* https://thelistenersclub.com/2021/09/17/nino-rotas-first-symphony-sweeping-cinematic-grandeur/
2 AZ Quotes. https://www.azquotes.com/quote/1551536
3 Filmmakingquotes (2022, December 22). *Post Production: Sound and Music Quotes.* https://filmmakingquotes.com/sound-and-music-quotes/
4 Eisenstein, Sergei (1968). *Film Essays and a Lecture.* Princeton University Press, p. 195.
5 Shostakovich, Dmitri (2004, January 1). *Testimony: The Memoirs of Dmitri Shostakovich.* Limelight Editions, p. 149.
6 CB14 (2013, July 23). "Edward Artemiev on Working for Andrei Tarkovsky". *YouTube.* https://www.youtube.com/watch?v=xjVT7MlE5rY

3

THE HISTORY OF MUSIC FOR ANIMATION

THE LEGACY OF WALT DISNEY

The name Disney is synonymous with animation. Since its inception in 1923, the company has received 135 Academy Awards, with the founder Walt Disney receiving 26 of them. Walt Disney Studios is the company's film-studio division, which today includes Walt Disney Pictures, Walt Disney Animation Studios, Marvel Studios, Lucasfilm, Pixar, 20th Century Studios, 20th Century Animation, and Searchlight Pictures. The company is said to have produced some of the greatest films ever made, not to mention revolutionizing the theme park industry.

From the earliest Disney animated films to the more recent live-action remakes, music has played a significant role in shaping popular culture for nearly a century. One of the key features of Disney music is its ability to create emotional connections between the audience and the characters and stories depicted on screen. Whether it's the infectious, upbeat tunes of *The Little Mermaid* (1989) or the sweeping orchestral themes of *The Lion King* (1994), Disney music has a way of capturing the spirit and energy of the films it accompanies, while birthing some of the most iconic and memorable songs in popular music history, from "When You Wish Upon a Star" to "Let It Go."

Explaining the importance of music in Disney's magic formula, Walt Disney once said:

> Music had always had a prominent part in all our products from the early cartoon days. So much so, in fact, that I cannot think of the pictorial story without thinking about the complementary music that will fulfill it. . . . I have had no formal musical training. But by long experience and by strong personal learning, I've selected musical themes, original or adapted, that were guided to wide audience acceptance.[1]

Disney has often incorporated different musical genres into its films, from the jazz-influenced *The Aristocats* (1970) to the Broadway-style showstoppers of *Beauty and the Beast* (1991) and *Frozen* (2013). By exposing children to a diverse

DOI: 10.4324/9781003289722-3

range of musical styles, Disney has helped to broaden their cultural horizons and inspire a lifelong love of music.

STEAMBOAT WILLIE

Early in its existence, Disney established itself as a leader in the animation industry through the creation of the popular character Mickey Mouse. As a test screening for the Mickey Mouse character, who would eventually become the company's mascot, the studio produced the silent films *Plane Crazy* and *The Galloping Gaucho* in May 1928. Later that year, the studio produced its first sound film, the third Mickey Mouse short, *Steamboat Willie*, which was the first sound cartoon to feature synchronized sound and music.

After the release of *Steamboat Willie*, Mickey Mouse became a character with immense popularity. Mickey and other characters appeared in a number of animated films produced by Disney Brothers Cartoon Studio. In August 1929, the company began collaborating with Columbia Pictures to create the *Silly Symphony* animated series. Carl W. Stalling, a former silent movie theater pianist, was instrumental in launching the series and composed the music for early films.

Carl Stalling's musical style was characterized by a frenetic, fast-paced, and highly eclectic approach, often featuring rapid shifts in mood, tempo, and musical style.

Stalling's music drew from a wide range of sources, including classical, jazz, popular music, and folk, as well as sound effects and other audio elements. He was particularly known for his use of musical quotations and references, often incorporating well-known melodies into his scores in unexpected ways. Stalling's music was also notable for its close synchronization with the on-screen action, with sound effects and musical cues often used to underscore visual gags and comedic moments. His style had a significant influence on the animated music that we hear today.

Stalling urged Disney to create a new series of animated short films in which the animation and action would be designed to complement the music. At the time, film music was composed to correspond with the action on screen once the picture was finished. The first of the Silly Symphonies, *The Skeleton Dance* (1929), was the first animated film in which the animation sequences were choreographed to pre-recorded music. This close synchronization of music and on-screen movement, which was popularized by these short films, became known as Mickey Mousing, a common film-scoring technique still in use today in both animated and narrative films.

The ability to synchronize music with the action in a film proved to be highly challenging, especially when recording live musicians. While at Disney, Stalling developed a system for scoring the music of animated films based on a "tick system." Each earphone-wearing musician in the orchestra recorded to a steady beat, much like a metronome. This allowed them to synchronize and record the music with more precise timing with the action on the screen. This recording technique is now commonly referred to as a click track and is also widely used in studios today.

DISNEY'S GOLDEN AGE

After Stalling left Disney to join Warner Bros., the studio hired two new composers, Frank Churchill and Leigh Harline. These two men would score and compose songs for some of the most iconic and successful Disney films, including *Snow White and the Seven Dwarfs*, *Pinocchio*, *Dumbo* (1941), and *Bambi* (1942).

Snow White and the Seven Dwarfs was an important film in the history of animation because it was the first full-length animated feature, as well as the first soundtrack album to be released commercially. When adjusted for inflation, it is one of the top ten highest earners in box-office history and the highest-grossing animated film of all time.

Composed by Churchill and Harline, the original score for *Snow White* features a variety of musical styles, including classical, folk, and popular music. Heavily influenced by the Golden Age Hollywood music innovated by Max Steiner, it makes ample use of leitmotifs associated with specific characters and situations in the film. Some of the notable themes in the score include Snow White's theme – a gentle and sweet melody that represents her innocence and kindness – the Queen's theme – a dark and ominous melody that represents her evil and menacing nature – the Seven Dwarfs' theme – a lively and playful melody captures their fun-loving and adventurous spirit – and the Love theme – a romantic melody that underlines the growing love between Snow White and the Prince. The score also features the songs "Heigh-Ho," "Whistle While You Work," and the iconic "Some Day My Prince Will Come," which was subsequently recorded by artists ranging from Barbra Streisand, Peggy Lee, and Linda Ronstadt, to jazz-legend Miles Davis.

It was the artistic achievement and commercial success of *Snow White* that introduced the animated feature-length film, thus beginning the Golden Era of Animation for Disney, which included films like *Cinderella*, *Peter Pan* (1953), *Lady and the Tramp* (1955), *Sleeping Beauty* (1959), *One Hundred and One Dalmatians* (1961), *The Jungle Book* (1967), *The Aristocats*, and *Bedknobs and Broomsticks* (1971).

In the long, sprawling legacy of Disney composers, a few names stand out. Originally hired as an arranger by Disney in 1953, George Bruns eventually became the music director who scored *Sleeping Beauty*, *One Hundred and One Dalmatians*, *The Jungle Book*, and *The Aristocats*. In addition to penning the beloved songs of *Mary Poppins* (1964), *Chitty Chitty Bang Bang* (1968), *The Jungle Book*, *Bedknobs and Broomsticks*, the team of Richard and Robert Sherman was responsible for "It's a Small World" for the theme park, which, according to *Time* magazine, maybe the most publicly performed song in history. Meanwhile, Oliver Wallace, who created scores and songs for *Alice in Wonderland* (1941), *Dumbo*, *Cinderella*, *Peter Pan*, and *Lady and the Tramp*, also wrote the titular song "Der Fuehrer's Face" from a 1942 propaganda cartoon starring Donald Duck. This parody was one of the most popular songs of the Second World War.

DISNEY DECLINE AND RENAISSANCE

Through the 1950s and 1960s, Walt Disney focused more on theme parks than on films, with the company producing an average of five feature films per year. After Walt Disney passed away in 1971, interest in animated films declined through the 1970s and into the mid-1980s, when the majority of the company's profits were coming from its theme parks. The Golden Age of Animation had ended.

The Disney Renaissance began when executives Michael Eisner and Jeffrey Katzenberg were hired (the two would eventually form DreamWorks with Steven Spielberg). During this period, from 1989 to 1999, a revitalized Walt Disney Animation produced critically and commercially successful films that were primarily musical adaptations of well-known stories, similar to those the studio produced during the 1930s and 1940s. The resurgence enabled Disney's animated films to become a domestic and international box-office powerhouse, earning significantly more money than the majority of Disney films from previous eras.

The Disney Renaissance began with the production of *The Little Mermaid* in 1989. Scored by Alan Menken, with lyrics by Harold Ashman, the film was a commercial success and won Academy Awards for Best Original Score and Best Original Song ("Under the Sea"). Alan Menken, who would go on to score and write original songs for *Beauty and the Beast*, *Aladdin* (1992), and *Pocahontas* (1995), was one of the most influential composers of this resurgent period for Disney, as well as more recent Disney films like *Enchanted* (2007), *Tangled* (2010), and *Disenchanted* (2022).

Having won eight Academy Awards, one Tony Award, 11 Grammys, and a Daytime Emmy Award, Menken is one of only 17 individuals to have earned "EGOT" status. Menken's musical style is marked by its broad appeal, strong melodic sensibility, and skillful combination of different musical genres and styles such as pop, rock, and Broadway-style musical theater. Of his approach to scoring animation, Menkin says:

> It's writing songs within the structure of telling a story, so it becomes a platform for diverse songwriting, for a writing process that's broader than just figuring out a song. You're also dealing with always pushing the story forward, with casting the voices, with the orchestration, with the arrangements.[2]

1992–94: ALADDIN AND THE LION KING

The Disney Renaissance also saw the release of *Aladdin* and *The Lion King*. At the time of its release, *Aladdin* was the highest-grossing animated film of all time, but it was later surpassed by *The Lion King*, which remains the highest-grossing traditionally animated film in history.

Swedish pop group ABBA was originally asked to compose the songs for *The Lion King* but declined the offer, leading Disney to hire Elton John to write the songs and Hans Zimmer to compose the score. Elton John played the piano and sang on many of the songs, infusing them with his unique voice and emotive performances. His song "Can You Feel the Love Tonight" won an Academy Award in 1994 for Best Original Song and a Grammy Award for Best Male Pop Vocal Performance. Of the experience, Zimmer said:

> One of the things people don't really realize in animation is you are dealing with a completely silent canvas, and you have to create a world, and you can create any world you want. I like this idea that you go somewhere to do your movie. One of the things

about *Lion King* was to actually go to South Africa and work with the real choirs. And it was really important that the first note was basically telling you you're not in Kansas anymore.[3]

In 1997, *The Lion King* was adapted into a Broadway stage musical, which has gone on to become the highest-grossing and third longest-running production in Broadway history.

PIXAR

In 1991, Disney signed a three-movie deal with computer animation studio Pixar to produce three feature films: *Toy Story* (1995), *A Bug's Life* (1998), and *Toy Story 2* (1999). Founded in 1979 as part of the Lucasfilm computer division known as the Graphics Group, Pixar Animation Studios broke off on its own in 1986 with funding from Apple co-founder Steve Jobs, who became its majority shareholder until Disney's ultimate acquisition in 1999.

Beginning with *Toy Story*, the first fully computer-animated feature-length film, Pixar has produced 26 feature-length films to date. While Disney wanted *Toy Story* to be a musical, having had great success incorporating Broadway-style musical numbers into their previous animated films, Pixar disagreed. As a compromise, the film would feature non-diegetic songs as background music, even though the characters would not sing, with singer-songwriter Randy Newman hired to compose the film's score and original songs, including the film's signature song, "You've Got a Friend in Me."

In the wake of *Toy Story*'s massive success (it was the highest-grossing film of 1995), Newman went on to compose the music for nine Disney-Pixar animated films, including three *Toy Story* sequels, *A Bug's Life*, both *Monsters, Inc.* films (2001, 2013), and the first and third *Cars* films (2006, 2017), as well as Disney's *James and the Giant Peach* (1996) and *The Princess and the Frog* (2009). Newman has been nominated for 22 Academy Awards in the categories of Best Original Score and Best Original Song, and has won twice in the latter category.

Another notable Pixar composer is Michael Giacchino, who scored seven Pixar films: *The Incredibles* (2004), *Ratatouille* (2007), *Up* (2009), *Cars 2* (2011), *Inside Out* (2015), *Coco* (2017), and *The Incredibles 2* (2018). He won an Oscar for his work on *Up* and three Grammys for his work on *Ratatouille* and *Up*. The musical style of these scores is based on both the animated scoring style of Carl Stalling as well as the big cinematic style of Max Steiner.

These movies were all commercially successful, and they established Pixar as a leader in the field of computer-generated animation. In 2006, Disney purchased Pixar for $7.4 billion, making it a wholly owned subsidiary of Disney.

FROZEN

Even with the purchase of Pixar, Disney continued to make their own animated films with a high degree of commercial success. In the 2000s, some notable Disney films included *Lilo & Stitch* (2002), *The Princess and the Frog* and *Wreck-it*

Ralph (2012), but it wasn't until *Frozen* that Disney would once again produce an animated musical blockbuster without Pixar.

Released in 2013, some film critics consider *Frozen* to be Disney's best-animated film since the studio's Renaissance period, praising its visuals, screenplay, themes, music, and voice acting. The music of *Frozen* was written and composed by the husband-and-wife songwriting team of Robert Lopez and Kristen Anderson-Lopez, whose musical numbers comprise approximately 23 minutes of the film.

Due to their residence in New York City, their close collaboration with the production team in Burbank required nearly daily, two-hour-long video conferences for approximately 14 months. For each song they composed, they recorded a demo in their home studio, and then emailed it to the team in Burbank for discussion during the following video conference. Lopez and Anderson-Lopez knew that their work would be compared to that of Alan Menken and Howard Ashman from the Disney Renaissance period. In the end, they composed 25 songs for the film, of which only eight were used.

Reflecting on their Oscar-winning work, Kristen Anderson-Lopez said:

> I think what inspired us to become part of this, what I really responded to, was that this was a story about sisters. It wasn't your traditional romance-would-solve-everything kind of story. It was about all the other parts of love and exploring other dimensions of love, while also getting your romantic love because that's an important part of life too.[4]

Back in 1936, the famous Broadway composer Jerome Kern set the stage for Disney's long, decorated legacy of music when he said, "Cartoonist Walt Disney has made the twentieth century's only important contribution to music. Disney has made use of music as language."[5]

WARNER BROS

Warner Bros. Cartoons, Inc. was an American animation studio that operated as the in-house animation division of Warner Bros. It was primarily responsible for the *Looney Tunes* and *Merrie Melodies* animated short-film series, making it one of the most successful animation studios in American media history. The cartoon characters in these series, which include Bugs Bunny, Daffy Duck, and Porky Pig, are among the most recognizable in the world.

Looney Tunes and *Merrie Melodies*, both introduced in the early 1930s, were Warner Bros.' two most influential early animated series. After Carl Stalling left Disney in 1930, he was hired by Warner Bros. in 1936, where he scored over 600 animated films until his retirement in 1958, averaging one score every week.

In much the same way as Max Steiner did for feature-length films, Carl Stalling invented the musical vocabulary and techniques for animated films. Contemporary composer John Zorn put it this way:

> Stalling was a visionary behind kaleidoscopic music that beat at the heart of the classic cartoons produced by Warner Bros. Studios in the mid-twentieth century, whose work deserves consideration among the best American avant-garde music ever recorded.

Frantic and passionate, his work opened new paths by following the visual trajectory of the action on screen instead of the accepted composition rules. . . . Stalling not only broke the rules, he made them irrelevant, since the melody, style and form collided in a glorious combination of sound and image. A rebel whose reach extended from pop to jazz, classical music and beyond, Stalling's revolutionary cutting and pasting compositions remain a clear precursor to experimental music created in its path. In fact, one could easily argue that he managed to introduce a whole generation of young cartoon fans to avant-garde music."[6]

Following the success of Walt Disney's *The Lion King,* Warner Bros. and several other Hollywood studios entered the feature animation game. The first of Warner's animated features was *Space Jam* (1996), a live-action/animated hybrid starring basketball star Michael Jordan and Bugs Bunny (Jordan had previously appeared in a number of Nike commercials with the *Looney Tunes*). They followed that with *The Iron Giant* (1999), by future Pixar director Brad Bird (*Ratatouille, The Incredibles*), which received widespread acclaim from critics and audiences.

Since 2007, Warner Bros. Animation has also produced the DC Universe Animated Original Movies, which are a series of animated superhero films based on the DC Comics characters and stories, including Batman, Superman, Suicide Squad, and the Justice League. The music to the DC series shares the dark, gritty, orchestral style of many of the feature films. The scores to *Batman: The Animated Series* (1992–95) and *Superman: The Animated Series* (1996–2000) were both composed by Shirley Walker, who not only set the tone for all the succeeding DC series but was one of the first female composers to be embraced by the Hollywood system.

HANNA-BARBERA

After creating the iconic *Tom and Jerry* shorts for MGM Studios in the 1940s, animation partners William Hanna and Joseph Barbera founded Hanna-Barbera Productions in 1957, after MGM stopped production on animated films. They found success in television early on with *The Huckleberry Hound Show,* which debuted on television in 1958. Over the next 30 years Hanna-Barbera produced an astounding 249 distinct animated television series, totaling over 1,200 hours of original episodes, including beloved cartoons like *Quick Draw McGraw* (1959), *The Flintstones* (1960), *Yogi Bear* (1961), *The Jetsons* (1962), *Jonny Quest* (1964), *Scooby-Doo* (1969), *Josie and the Pussycats* (1970), *Super Friends* (1973), and *The Smurfs* (1981).

Composer and music producer Hoyt Curtin was the mastermind behind the majority of Hanna-Barbera's iconic music, penning the immortal theme songs for television classics such as *The Flintstones, The Jetsons, Scooby-Doo, Josie and the Pussycats,* and *The Smurfs.* Curtin began his music career as a trombonist and arranger for big bands, and his compositional style was heavily influenced by the jazz, big band, and swing music of the 1930s and 1940s, which he often incorporated into his compositions. Curtin also experimented with various genres and styles, incorporating rock, country, and classical elements into his work.

In the late 1950s, television animation blossomed, and, given the short production times and smaller budgets needed to produce a larger number of episodes, the storylines became dialogue-driven rather than action-based. Thus, television animation moved away from the previously popular slapstick comedy style and more toward the studio sitcom format of the time. Accordingly, music made the same transition away from the tightly synced style of early Disney and Warner cartoons, where the music choreographed every gesture and movement, to supplying a general mood instead. One of the reasons for the change of cartoon style scoring was that there was simply not enough time to compose and record a tightly synchronized score due to the faster production schedule of television. Hoyt Curtain would often be scoring eight to ten individual cartoon series simultaneously.

The musical style of the Warner Bros. and Hanna-Barbera animated television series would go on to have a big influence on the music of shows like *The Simpsons* and *Family Guy*. *Simpsons* creator Matt Groening recalls how his own show's theme music came together:

> At the very beginning when we were trying to figure out how the show was supposed to sound, I made a mixtape of my favorite cartoon music. Hoyt Curtin who did the Hanna-Barbera cartoon music. I loved the *Jetsons* theme the best. We hooked up with Danny Elfman of Oingo Boingo, who had just started to do his film composing.[7]

Danny Elfman, who at that time was known as the frontman of surrealist New Wave band Oingo Boingo, remembers it similarly:

> I got called into a meeting with Matt Groening. He showed me a pencil sketch of the opening of *The Simpsons* and it felt very retro and crazy, what I remember growing up on. I told him, 'If you want something contemporary, I'm not the guy for that. But if you want something like a crazy Hanna-Barbera that never was, then I think I'm the right guy.' I literally wrote the piece in the car on my way home from the meeting. . . . Then I sent the cassette back to Matt, and I think I got a call the next day saying, 'Yeah, that's it.' . . . I didn't know that I would actually be hitting a jackpot. I didn't expect anybody to see *The Simpsons*. I didn't think it would last more than one season, if it even lasted one season. I did it purely for fun. That silly moment would become this major defining moment in my life.

STUDIO GHIBLI

Founded in 1985 by directors Hayao Miyazaki and Isao Takahata and producer Toshio Suzuki, Japan's Studio Ghibli is responsible for some of the most beautiful and original animation of the last 40 years. The studio was established following the success of Miyazaki's film *Nausicaä of the Valley of the Wind* (1984). Miyazaki chose the name Ghibli from the Italian noun 'ghibli,' derived from the Libyan Arabic word for hot desert wind (ghiblī), with the intention of breathing new life into the anime industry.

Studio Ghibli is best known for its animated feature films, but it has also created a number of shorts, television commercials, and two television films. Totoro, a giant spirit inspired by raccoon dogs – and title character of 1988's *My Neighbor Totoro* – serves as the organization's mascot and most recognizable symbol. Their most beloved and top-grossing films include *Princess Mononoke* (1997), *Spirited Away* (2001), *Howl's Moving Castle* (2004), and *Ponyo* (2008).

Composer Mamoru Fujisawa, also known as Joe Hisaishi, composed the music for almost all of Studio Ghibli's films; a collaboration that began in 1983 when Hisaishi was tasked with creating the score for *Nausicaä of the Valley of the Wind*. Miyazaki was so impressed by Hisaishi's work that the two became fast friends, resulting in one of the longest-lasting collaborations in film history, on par with Spielberg and John Williams.

Dubbed "the John Williams of Japan" by Pitchfork, Hisaishi has over 100 film scores and solo albums to his name, winning the Japanese Academy Award for Best Music seven times. Hisaishi's music often blends elements of traditional Japanese music with Western classical music and contemporary popular music. This fusion of styles creates a unique sound that is both familiar and fresh. He is known for his ability to write memorable melodies that are often simple and easy to sing along with. His melodies are often influenced by Japanese folk music and are typically played by a solo instrument or a small ensemble. Along with his use of solo instruments, his music is primarily symphonic, featuring orchestral arrangements that are lush and full.

Explaining his mindset when scoring, Joe Hisaishi says:

> Basically, most of my music is for Japanese cinema, but when I compose film music I constantly try to work at a 'world level', thinking that people from all over the world will be watching the film with my music. For example, I'm concerned about the reactions of foreign musicians who watch the film to how I use the orchestra and instruments. I always create music from an objective point of view. How the world will react to this point of view is an important consideration for me as I compose music.[8]

DREAMWORKS ANIMATION

DreamWorks Animation was founded as a division of DreamWorks Pictures in 1994, but in 2004 it became an independent company before being acquired by NBC Universal in 2016. After previously producing traditionally animated and stop-motion films such as *The Prince of Egypt* (1998) and *Wallace & Gromit: The Curse of the Were-Rabbit* (2005), the studio now relies solely on computer animation, which it has used to create multi-film franchises like *Shrek* (2001), *Madagascar* (2005), *Kung Fu Panda* (2008), and *How to Train Your Dragon* (2010).

DreamWorks Animation scores often mix traditional orchestral music with electronic elements, creating a modern and dynamic sound. Many DreamWorks films feature sweeping melodies and epic themes, which help to convey a sense of adventure and wonder.

It is no coincidence that one of the pioneers of this orchestral-electronic hybrid score, Hans Zimmer, who is currently the head of their film-music division, has scored 12 animated films for DreamWorks. Meanwhile, John Powell is responsible for the Celtic-inspired scores in the *How to Train Your Dragon* films, in addition to co-scoring *Antz* (1998), *Chicken Run* (2000) and *Shrek* with Harry Gregson-Williams.

CHAPTER SUMMARY

- The 1928 Disney short *Steamboat Willie* was the first fully synchronized original score.
- The tight synchronicity between music and score is called *Mickey Mousing*.
- Considered one of the most influential composers of all time, Carl Stalling was an important composer for early Disney and Looney Tunes animations.
- Disney's *Snow White and the Seven Dwarfs* was the first feature-length animated musical and one of the highest-grossing films of the time.
- Hanna-Barbera brought animation to television during the 1960s, 1970s, and 1980s with the iconic music of Hoyt Curtain.
- Studio Ghibli raised the status of animated films to narrative filmmaking, with music composed by Joe Hiashasi.
- Pixar, DreamWorks, and Disney remain as some of the top animated film studios in the world.

NOTES

1 Continuation of a Disney Discography. *Walt Disney and Music – In His Own Words.* http://bjbear71.com/Disney/Walt_and_Music.html#:~:text=%22Music%20had%20always%20had%20a,had%20no%20formal%20musical%20training

2 Brainyquote.   https://www.brainyquote.com/authors/alan-menken-quotes#:~:text=It's%20writing%20songs%20within%20the,the%20orchestration%2C%20with%20the%20arrangements

3 Elegyscores (2014, September 25). "Hans Zimmer – Scoring the Lion King Interview". *YouTube.* https://www.youtube.com/watch?v=hGxdrwhtxAY

4 DP/30: The Oral History of Hollywood (2013, November 21). "Frozen Songwriters Kristen Anderson-Lopez, Robert Lopez". *YouTube.* https://www.youtube.com/watch?v=DY-NMbZ4Z2M

5 Jerome   Kern   Quotefancy.   https://quotefancy.com/quote/1744281/Jerome-Kern-Cartoonist-Walt-Disney-has-made-the-twentieth-century-s-only-important

6 John Zorn (2020, February 24). "Carl Stalling Project". *Facebook.* https://www.facebook.com/groups/6660861756/posts/10158274383226757/

7 LA Phil (2014, September 6). "Matt Groening on How the Simpsons Theme Was Influenced by Carl Stalling and Other Great Composers". *YouTube* https://www.youtube.com/watch?v=-UthzUr0rFQ

8 Schilling, Mark "Interview With Joe Hisaishi". *Far East Film Festival.* https://www.fareast-film.com/eng/archive/catalogue/2015/intervista-con-joe-hisaishi/?IDLYT=31711

4

THE LANGUAGE OF FILM MUSIC

INTRODUCTION

What makes a great film score? Is the language of film music different or separate from the language of popular music, from songwriting, from EDM, or from classical music? Is its language determined by what we see as much as by what we hear, or is film music expected to live outside the film? Is the quality of the film music better if we can hear the progression of the story in the music alone, or is supplying a mood enough for it to be valued? These are the questions that every filmmaker and film composer grapples with.

Whatever answers we may come up with for these questions, one thing remains certain: when image and music are played together, they are unified into something new, something bigger, something more expressive and expansive than the sum of their parts. The French music theorist Michel Chion eloquently states: "one perception influences the other and transforms it. We never see the same thing when we also hear; we don't hear the same thing when we see as well."[1]

John Williams echoes this point:

> When we watch films, I don't think we separate one thing from another. When we listen to the dialogue, we hear sound effects and we hear an orchestra or whatever music it is. But I don't think we take it apart as we listen to it. We can discuss the elements technically or clinically after the fact, but when we experience the film, it's the totality that moves us or doesn't move us. I think music's role is to become part of the living body of the film. We need the music to be there.

All of us can agree that music adds a certain magic to what we are looking at and, from what has been covered in previous chapters, how the type of music (or lack of music) moves films on a scale from the realistic to the fantastical. The style of the film depends on the amount and type of music used. *Star Wars* creates its fantasy universe by using an epic Golden Age orchestral score that plays continuously from beginning to end. This score is essential to create the suspension of disbelief needed for us to enjoy the fantasy elements. George Lucas said:

DOI: 10.4324/9781003289722-4

The *Star Wars* films are basically silent movies and they're designed as silent movies therefore the music has a very large role in carrying the story more than it would in a normal movie.[2]

Lucas' perspective indicates the huge influence that music can have on the dramatic development of a film. By contrast, one of the characteristics of the French New Wave was the rebellion against this type of filmmaking and a return to a documentary-like cinematic realism by using very little music, and when music is used, it is made to sound like the music is being heard by the characters, rather than a background score that is commenting on what the audience is seeing.

TYPES OF FILM MUSIC

There are three types of film sound, or, said another way, three different ways that music can interact with film: *diegetic, non-diegetic*, and *metadiegetic*. Diegetic sound refers to everything that can be heard by characters in the film. Non-diegetic sound, by contrast, cannot be heard by the characters but only by the audience, and metadiegetic is sound or music that only a specific character hears.

DIEGETIC MUSIC

Diegetic music is also known as source music, which is any music that comes from the world of the film. This is most commonly the music that the characters are listening to in a scene or performing as musical instrumentalists. The very first sound in film was diegetic music, with Al Jolson playing the role of a singer in *The Jazz Singer*. With diegetic music, the audience is aware that the music playing is what the characters are hearing.

Some other popular examples of diegetic music include: the cantina band in *Star Wars*, Davy Jones's playing the organ in *Pirates of the Caribbean* (2003), John Travolta and Uma Thurman dancing to Chuck Berry's "You Never Can Tell" in *Pulp Fiction* (1994), Lady Gaga and Bradley Cooper singing together in *A Star Is Born* (2018), and the string quartet playing dance music at the grand balls in *Bridgerton*.

Movie musicals, in which the natural storyline is broken to accommodate a song and dance number, are an interesting type of diegetic music. When Simba sings "Hakuna Matata," does he hear the backing tracks? Does Elsa hear the orchestra while singing "Let it Go"? In both cases, we do not see musicians performing but they are an integral part of the music that the characters are singing. These questions have led film-music theorists to coin the term *unreal diegetic music*, as opposed to *real diegetic*, which bridges the worlds of diegetic music and score.

NON-DIEGETIC MUSIC

Non-Diegetic music is the term used for what we commonly think of as a musical score. It is the music that only we, the audience, can hear. This music is not part of the character's world, and filmmakers use non-diegetic music to establish the tone, mood, and atmosphere of a film, and to enhance the emotions of the viewers. Non-diegetic music includes both original scoring and songs. This is the music that score composers are hired to write, whether it's an orchestral score like *Thor* (2011), an electronic score like *Ex Machina* (2014), or an experimental score like *Arrival*.

Some popular examples of non-diegetic music include the two-note shark theme in *Jaws*, the entire score of *Star Wars*, the song "I Will Always Love You" from *The Bodyguard* (1992), "My Heart Will Go On" from *Titanic*, and the scores to not only *The Lord of the Rings* and the Marvel movies, but all background music, from action and comedy to period romance and documentaries.

METADIEGETIC MUSIC

The third type of sound and music in film is called metadiegetic, which is music or sound that can only be heard by a particular character or characters in the film. An example of meta-diegetic sound is the music that plays inside a character's head, or the loss of hearing or ringing in the ears after a big explosion in action movies.

Some examples of metadiegetic music include the music Maximus hears at the end of *Gladiator* (2000) as he approaches his wife and son, Joaquin Phoenix dancing on the stairs in *Joker* (2019), Salieri looking through Mozart's scores and hearing the music in his mind in *Amadeus* (1984), and Eminem writing rap lyrics while riding the bus in *8 Mile* (2002).

FILM MUSIC COMPONENTS

The score is a central component of a film and can be seen as the film's emotional pulse. It is what propels the film forward, and can bring us to tears or terrify us. As James Cameron tells it:

> The score is the heartbeat of the film, and that can be literal. It can be the rhythm, it can be the thing that's propelling the film and making you feel like, 'Oh, my God, these characters are in danger.' You're racing along at high speed, or it can be the slow kind of emotional heart of the film. You'll associate it with characters. Sometimes the score sucks you right in through the character's eyes, inside their minds, and what they're feeling in a moment. You put that together with great acting, and you are having an emotional response. So the score is the heart and the soul of the film.[3]

How does music achieve this power and magic? Let us explore the components of film music to find out.

There are five main components of film music:

- Style – the genre and location of the music.
- Emotion – what the audience feels from the music.
- Energy Level – how much activity the music has.
- Timing – how the music is synchronized to the visual image.
- Form – how the music is organized.

These five components do not operate independently, but are rather interrelated. The relationship and intersection of these five components create the emotional power and unique musical world of each film. Let us take a look at them individually.

STYLE

Even though film music can contain different genres of music, film music itself is not a genre. It is a category of all musical components in a film. Musical genres can inform us about the setting of the film and give us insights into the filmmaker's intentions. A score's musical style can refer to a genre, a geographical location, or a location in time. For example, when we hear EDM in the cave rave scene from *The Matrix Reloaded* (2003) we intuitively associate that genre as modern, contemporary, or possibly futuristic. When we hear string quartet and the harpsichord in *Bridgerton* (2020), we assume an earlier historical period. Not only do we listen to the *Bridegerton* soundtrack and understand that it is a period drama, but we also know it's European, and specifically in an upper-class setting of that time and place.

The traditional classical style is also what informs us of the location in time when we watch period films like *Pride and Prejudice* (2005) or *Sense and Sensibility* (1995), in the same way that Daft Punk's synthesizer-driven score to *Tron Legacy* (2010) transports us to the future. In discussing his film *Mean Streets* (1973), Martin Scorsese addresses the importance of the music reflecting the time and place of the characters:

> The music that I was using was part of the world in which the characters live. They echo. I would hear them echoing through the hallways and the streets and the windows and car radios. And it was like a physical, as well as mental, architecture of the world I was trying to create, and in a way the music I chose . . . inspired me for certain scenes and certain films.[4]

From the sweeping Arabic desert music of *Lawrence of Arabia* (1962) to the Celtic flute of *Titanic*, the music signals to us the geographical location of the film, as well as its location in time. In the two above cases, the music signals specific locations in the world, and that same Celtic flute from *Titanic* (1997) can be heard in the Shire music of *The Fellowship of the Ring* (2001), where it transports us to the pastoral landscape of the imaginary world of the film. Though the Shire is a purely fictitious place, we know from the music that it is Irish or European-like, and not located, for instance, in the remote jungles of Africa.

Filmmakers can also use musical style in more unexpected ways, such as how, in HBO's *Westworld* (2016–2022), Ramin Djawadi uses an old-timey piano straight out of an Old West saloon to cover popular songs by Radiohead, Nirvana, and The Rolling Stones. Explaining how he came to reinterpret hits by Taylor Swift, Madonna, and Rihanna with a classical string quartet, *Bridgerton* composer Kris Bowers says:

> From what they said in that first meeting, [*Bridgerton*] is not your typical Regency era television show. It's set in 1813, but they wanted it to feel fresh and modern. And as they said, they didn't want it to feel like your grandmother's Regency television show. They wanted it to sound very unexpected for the time.[5]

EMOTION

Ever since motion pictures were invented, music has played a huge role in bring-ing a deeper emotional depth to the films we watch. In the words of Jerry Goldsmith, who wrote scores to *Planet of the Apes* (1968), *The Omen* (1976), and *Alien* (1979):

> Music is the most emotional of all the art forms, it reaches depths that no other form of art can reach. . . . Music for the screen serves a lot of functions. But the basic func-tion is to reinforce the emotional, the unseen element on the screen.[6]

Steven Spielberg echoes these thoughts and adds how John Williams' music shapes our emotions in his films:

> John's music directs all the traffic of our emotions. So when a staggering performance fills our eyes with tears, the appropriate score can make them fall. That's what fills us with wonder . . . and that's where E.T. got his soul.[7]

The tone of the music is not independent of the visual image. In film, the emo-tion depends not only on the piece of music we hear, but on the synchronicity of tone between what we see and what we hear. A beautiful, slow-string melody will evoke different responses depending on what is taking place on the screen. It may evoke hope in the ending of a romance, tragedy in a battle sequence, or possibly outright laughter due to its overly dramatic nature in a comedy.

Music has two ways to relate to the visual image. It can be in synchronicity with the film and reinforce the emotion we are seeing, which is called an *empa-thetic* relationship. Or it can play against the image, producing an inappropriate emotional response that is in contrast to the interpretation of what we are seeing, called an *anempathetic* relationship.

EMPATHETIC

The terms empathetic and anempathetic were coined by French composer and film theorist Michel Chion, who says:

> There are two ways for music in film to create a specific emotion in relation to the situation depicted on the screen. On one hand, music can directly express its partici-pation in the feeling of the scene. In this case we can speak of empathetic music, from the word empathy, the ability to feel the feelings of others. On one hand, music can directly express its participation in the feeling of the scene, by taking on the scene's rhythm, tone, and phrasing; obviously such music participates in cultural codes for things like sadness, happiness, and movement. In this case we can speak of empa-thetic music, from the word empathy, the ability to feel the feelings of others.[8]

Music can have an empathetic relationship with the on-screen images by being spe-cific to the visual action, to the emotion of the character, or provide a general mood or emotional tone to the image. In *Star Wars*, the iconic "Force theme" can be heard when Luke or Rey are moving objects with their minds. We hear what we can't see; the power of the Force visually and the musical motif associated with that power.

The Force theme can also be heard as the young Luke Skywalker looks off into the binary sunset, contemplating whether to stay on his uncle's moisture farm or take part in the adventure with Obi-Wan. Though we only see him looking out into the desert, the playing of the Force theme tells us what he has decided emotionally.

Music can also convey a general mood or tone, not only through its use of specific melodies but also by the style of the score itself. The sultry, jazzy brass of the James Bond films lets us always know that we are part of an action-packed world of sophistication and intrigue, whether he is sipping a shaken martini or chasing a spy on a Vespa through the alleys of Venice. We can also recognize the sadistic world of *Saw* (2004) by its industrial, ear-bleeding score by Charlie Clouser. As the first *Saw* movie opens in the black with a short voice-over, the mood is carried by ominous music that informs us that, although we don't know what is happening, it can't be good.

ANEMPATHETIC

Chion continues with his description of an anempathetic relationship:

> On the other hand, music can also exhibit conspicuous indifference to the situation, by progressing in a steady, undaunted, and ineluctable manner: the scene takes place against this very backdrop of 'indifference.' This juxtaposition of scene with indifferent music has the effect not of freezing emotion but rather of intensifying it, by inscribing it on a cosmic background. I call this second kind of music anempathetic.[9]

Anempathetic music is also known as *counterpoint* in the world of film, which is not to be mistaken with the same musical term. In film, contrapuntal music is a technique in which a series of independent musical and film parts are pieced together in a harmonious manner, such that it produces a deeper narrative meaning. Director Spike Lee explains:

> One thing I think that people might not understand is what you call juxtaposition, where the music doesn't have to necessarily be the same feeling as what you are seeing on screen. It might be a contrast exactly to what you're gonna see. . . . The term is called counterpoint, where the music gives you is opposite of what you feel.[10]

There are a number of interesting ways that anempathetic music can influence our emotional reactions to what we are viewing. The most common way is through foreshadowing, where an audience is prepared for an upcoming event by presenting music that suggests the future course of activities is uncertain. Foreshadowing very commonly occurs at the opening of many films. One great example is in the opening to Stanley Kubrick's *The Shining* (1980), when we see a car driving through a scenic country road somewhere in the Rocky Mountains. What would, on its own, be a beautiful and serene landscape, is undermined by the ominous music from the requiem "Dies Irae," which signals to the audience that, underneath this pastoral serenity, evil is brewing. By doing so, the audience is drawn into the film and invited to generate expectations about what will happen next.

Another emotional response is extreme dramatization, where the wrong music exaggerates the emotions of a scene. An iconic example of extreme dramatization is the use of the slow orchestral "Adagio for Strings" in the death scene of Willem Dafoe's character Sergeant Elias in *Platoon* (1986). Sergeant Elias is running through the jungles of Vietnam being pursued by the enemy with explosions and gunshots all around him. Instead of the common fast-paced action score, which would ratchet up the excitement and anticipation of whether he will make it or not, all sound is muted except for the slow, soul-stirring string orchestra. This not only anticipates his imminent death, but underpins the senseless struggle and tragedy of the lives lost in war. A more recent example is from *Inception*, where Édith Piaf's song "Non, je ne regrette rien" is slowed down and played while the van falls off the bridge in slow motion, characterizing the "dream within a dream" subtext of the film.

The anempathetic relationship also can function to dehumanize a character, such as the use of the Hollywood show tune "Singing in the Rain" during the brutal rape scene in *A Clockwork Orange*, or when the Beach Boys' "Good Vibrations" plays as the protagonist is killed in the Jordan Peele horror film *Us* (2019). The dehumanization can even border on the comical, such as when the 1970s earworm "Stuck in the Middle with You" soundtracks the famous ear-cutting scene from *Reservoir Dogs* (1992), or how in *Dr. Strangelove* (1964) the Vera Lynn song "We'll Meet Again" is played as Slim Pickens rides a nuclear bomb headed toward Earth, signaling the end of humanity. The wrong music can also just bring a fun chuckle to a film like *Shaun of the Dead* (2004), where Queen's song "Don't Stop Me Now" plays over a zombie-killing frenzy, or even the fun gypsy violin solo accompanying Dredger's attempt to kill Robert Downey Jr. in Guy Ritchie's *Sherlock Holmes* (2009).

SUBTEXT

The way that many composers look at the synchronicity between musical emotion and the emotion of the images is in terms of subtext. Subtext includes the thoughts and emotions that lie beyond the characters' words or the images shown. Every story has multiple character arcs that make up the larger dramatic story. Every character has a backstory and a psychological world independent from what we may actually see. An interesting example of the power of subtext in music is Hans Zimmer's score to *Interstellar*. As Zimmer tells it:

> So I run into [Christopher Nolan] and he goes, 'Listen, if I were to write something, just a letter with a metaphorical story that had nothing to do with the movie,' and he would never tell me what the movie was about, would I give him a day and just write whatever came to me? This letter arrived with this beautiful story about what it meant to be a father. And so I spent a day writing. So he came over and he sat down on the couch, and I said, 'Okay, I'll play it to you.' And I played him this fragile little piece that I'd written about my son . . . and I get to the end of it, and I'm going, 'So what do you think?' [Nolan says,] 'Well, I better make the movie then.' I'm like, 'What is the movie?' And he started talking about space and huge and epic and all this. Then finally, I'm going, 'Stop, stop. I've written this tiny, tiny little thing.' You know, this really fragile personal thing. And he goes, 'Yes, I know where the heart of the movie is now.'[11]

The piece Zimmer is referring to is called "Day One" on the *Interstellar* soundtrack. From that small and delicate piano piece, which follows the subtext of the father and daughter's relationship, became one of the most epic science fiction masterpieces of the 21st century.

Expanding on the role of subtext, Zimmer continues:

> There is a subtext because you don't want to go and tell the story that [the filmmaker is] telling beautifully, elegantly in images and words. You want to go and slip in underneath and find that bit that they are not illuminating yet. That takes the whole thing just one step further into sometimes the metaphysical world, sometimes into a more emotional world, or sometimes just figuring out how to color a scene in a slightly different way.[12]

ENERGY LEVEL

The energy level is defined by the amount of musical activity in a scene or film. This activity creates the intensity of emotional energy that we feel when we listen. The energy level has four components:

- Rhythmic activity.
- Harmonic activity.
- Melodic activity.
- Timbre/volume.

Elaborating on the importance of the emotional intensity, James Cameron says:

> The music drives the emotion of the film. It drives the propulsion. It creates feelings of tension, or beauty, or melancholy if that's what the scene requires, if that's what you need to be feeling at that point. It's absolutely critical. All your other work on a film can come to nothing if you don't get the music right.[13]

RHYTHMIC ACTIVITY

Overall rhythmic activity in a composition is determined by the tempo and the rhythmic subdivision. The tempo is the speed of the beat, and the rhythmic subdivision is how many parts the beat is divided into. The speed of the music is also known as the tempo, which is measured in beats per minute, or BPM. The faster the BPM, the more intensity we feel. Low-energy music is characterized by a slower tempo and fewer rhythmic subdivisions, giving the impression of a lower level of rhythmic activity. The rhythmic activity in high-energy music is generated by a faster tempo and the addition of more rhythmic subdivisions.

As the tempo speeds up, the musical intensity builds. In the words of composer Charlie Clouser, speaking about his score to *Saw*:

> The tempo starts this section at 137 [BPM] and works its way all the way up to 146. It's gradually, every couple of bars, it's going up, one or two beats per minute. As all the strings keep rising in pitch, the tempo is gradually getting faster . . . everything's going crazy, our heads are about to explode.[14]

Clouser highlights the correspondence between the speed of the tempo increasing and the strings rising in pitch as an example of how the two musical parameters work together. Action films demand a faster tempo to keep pace with the excitement of the visual image. The faster tempos also demand more musical activity, using subdivisions and having to put more notes per page. As John Williams explains:

> A film like *Star Wars* or *The Empire Strikes Back* is generally active music. It's fast, the tempos are quick, there are a lot of flourishing in the orchestra, and so on. It's notey, so that it's a tremendous physical job of just getting the notes down.[15]

HARMONIC ACTIVITY

The harmonic activity can be based on the types of chords being used, the relationship between the chords (i.e. chord progression), and the speed at which the chords change. In the shower scene from Alfred Hitchcock's *Psycho* (1960), composer Bernard Herrmann uses very dissonant chords repeated to convey the sense of horror and shock. In *Vertigo* (1958), Herrmann uses slightly unusual chords that change every measure to give us a sense of discomfort, which helps us experience the physical sensation of vertigo that the character, Scotty, feels. In the same film, Herrmann uses traditional, late-romantic harmonies for the "Scene D'Amour" love music representing Jimmy Stewart's love obsession with Kim Novak. These kinds of harmonies and chord progressions can also be found in the operas of Wagner or the early film scores of Max Steiner, which inspire the familiar feeling of romance.

Furthermore, the universal meaning of these harmonies allows film music to convey specific emotions across cultures. As John Williams explains:

> Acculturation and tastes for European and Western harmony, this developed our sense of what's pretty, what isn't, what's ominous, or what's threatening, and so on ... but it's also connected with verifiable universalisms that exist in music that don't in language.[16]

Outside of the use of specific chords and chord progressions is the rate at which they change, called harmonic rhythm. A great example of the dramatic use of harmonic rhythm is at the end of *Dunkirk*. The entirety of Hans Zimmer's score consists of very fast rhythmic music with fast-paced chord changes, beginning slowly and accelerating as the movie progresses, to keep a single rise of tension for over an hour. Rather than being an uplifting culmination of what's come before, the very last cue is the opposite: a fast, upbeat heroic fanfare. In fact, it is a famous classical piece called "Nimrod" by Edward Elgar, which is played so painfully slow, at 6 BPM, that it can barely be recognized. Zimmer's co-composer Ben Wallfisch explains:

> 'Nimrod' has such meaning, especially for British people. It's often played at state events, or sometimes funerals, but the opportunity to actually slow that music right down and examine every harmony, and sort of experience each chord for its full emotional impact in the context of a score, which prior to that is all about not enabling you

to exhale, it's a constant sense of acceleration and upping of tension, is a real study of attention. So that moment, just to breathe and have that single G and an E flat major chord, is so different from everything we've had before. It's a sense of release and relief. And that was all about, yes, just making time stand still.[17]

MELODIC ACTIVITY

Note choices in the melody also influence the energy level and emotion of the music. In this realm, *consonant notes* are notes that are contained in the harmony, while *dissonant notes* are notes outside of the harmony. The interplay between consonance and dissonance in the melody creates its own emotional intensity and energy.

Dissonance resolving to consonance is the tension and release of musical energy. The opening of Hans Zimmer's piece "Time," from *Inception*, is melodically neutral given that all the notes of the melody are chord tones. As melodic lines are added to the opening texture through each repetition of the phrase, they become more active because dissonant notes are heard in those added melodies that resolve to consonant tones. At the very end of "Time," the French horn is added, playing dissonant notes that do not resolve to a consonant tone, which amplifies the emotional energy at the end.

Another excellent example of this tension-release of dissonance-consonance is in the "One Ring" theme in *The Fellowship of the Ring*. "The Ring" theme begins at the very opening of the film, from the title card through the story of forging the rings of power. The dissonance of the very first note of the violin melody creates an air of mystery and awe.

Oftentimes, composers also use melodic lines that are all dissonant, which is called *atonal music*. Atonal music is what is commonly heard in horror, thrillers, and scarier aspects of fantasy. The alternation between traditional music, which is called tonal, and tense atonal music allows composers to sculpt the emotional intensity over time. John Williams describes his score to Spielberg's *A.I. Artificial Intelligence* (2001):

The music is quite schizophrenic, at least in my mind, because you have very tonal aspects and some strings in the beginning. You have the piano at the end, then there are sections that are very atonal, which is to say dissonant or without the gravity of the tonal system to root it.[18]

TIMBRE

The quality or color of the sound itself is enough to enhance or diminish the energy level and our emotional reaction. This quality is known as timbre. The timbre can be of individual instruments, like John Williams' low and menacing string motif in *Jaws* and Mica Levi's unusual sound processing of the viola in *Under the Skin* (2013), or it can be the scraping metallic sounds of *Saw*.

A great example of using a timbre to represent a character, rather than a theme, can be found in *The Dark Knight* (2008). In his signal for the Joker, Hans Zimmer takes a single note in a solo cello and slowly moves it upwards, creating one of the tensest and most innovative uses of a single rising pitch to characterize the villain. Zimmer recalls:

> I thought, what if I can define a character in one note – actually it's two notes that clash beautifully with each other – and make it really like a taught string that gets tighter and tighter but never breaks. Ultimately it was the cello that did it.[19]

This method of working is in stark contrast to a traditional villain theme like the "Imperial March" from *The Empire Strikes Back* (1980), which signals the approach of Darth Vader. Both examples function in a similar way, associating a sound with a character, but use two very different methods. One is a theme performed with sound that we recognize, and the other is the recognition of the sound itself.

The use of timbre to create emotion can even extend to the use of noise or found sounds, which function as a primary building-block of the score. Composer Charlie Clouser describes an instrument built from scrap metal used in *Saw*:

> This is the instrument called Kaylasta, which was built by Chas Smith. . . . It's used in all the *Saw* horror movies, and because it's made out of rusty bits of scrap metal that sort of fits the ethos of those movies, it's become kind of a signature sound in all the *Saw* movies, and certain sounds conjure up a whole kind of emotional response.[20]

Thinking about the timbre of sound as an expressive parameter, away from specific musical instruments, has led composers into a completely new sound world. Clouser continues:

> I've always been fascinated by instruments that have an element of chaos and unsteadiness, and they can be manipulated to put them in pitch with a piece of music you're writing, but they're hard to control or on the edge of being atonal.[21]

TIMING

Film is an art form that evolves over time, and the pace of the images creates its own tempo and rhythm. The level of conformity between visual and musical events can be referred to as timing. We have already discussed the synchronicity of tone, which is the relationship between the mood of the music and the mood of the image. Along with a synchronicity of tone, there is also a synchronicity of timing, which is when events happen in the music that correspond to visual events. Or, as John Williams says:

> Starting first and foremost, with all things in film, is rhythm; it's all timing. It's not so much what you do before the eye, it's when you do it.[22]

The score can be tightly synchronized or loosely synchronized to the picture, and the level of concurrence between sound and visual events not only influences our emotional response to the film, but gives us clues about its style and genre. *Toy Story* composer Randy Newman discusses how stylistic references are inferred by the level of sync:

> In animation of course it matters, because you've got to hit everything or it looks funny. But in the straight pictures if you hit everything, it looks funny too. Tom Hanks falls down. You don't want to go *doom-doom* for him. But you want to hit something.[23]

The first films to feature sound were animated, and in that style of animation, music and picture are very tightly synchronized. This can be seen in the first animated scores Carl Stalling did for Disney. Animation has always tended to have a tighter level of sync between sound and image, because the musical score was often used as sound effects and the sound effects were recorded at the orchestral recording sessions.

We have now come to expect this style of scoring when watching animated films. Beginning with Disney's *Steamboat Willie* and Warner Bros' Bugs Bunny cartoons, tight timing became part of the style of animated scoring. As discussed before, this technique is called Mickey Mousing and is still used today in modern animated narrative films such as *Toy Story*, *Ice Age* (2002), *The Incredibles*, and *Ratatouille*.

It is important to remember that timing is an aspect of the film's style itself. The pace of the score is achieved by how closely the timing corresponds to what we are seeing. We notice the score more when the timings are tightly correlated to the film's action, and when the sync is looser the music fades into the background. Speaking on the varying degrees of synchronization, Danny Elfman refects:

> Obviously, not all pictures take a lot of synchronization. There's beautiful scores that don't actually hit a lot of action. And then we've got superhero movies and animation movies, where you're hitting a lot all the time. 'How does one do it?' is a really difficult question.[24]

You can imagine the difficulty of film-score composing due to the fact that the film edits create their own rhythm, which needs to coordinate with the tempo and rhythm of the music being composed. John Williams discusses the importance of finding the rhythm of the film:

> For me, the first thing is the rhythm of the film, and then character, texture and style, and all the other endless elements that go into it.[25]

Hans Zimmer continues:

> The drummer for the film composer is the editor, so you need to know your editor and you need to know how your editor feels tempo. You want to know the metabolism rate of your editor, because they're your drummer.[26]

There are three basic ways that composers can make the timings of the music correspond to the hit points in the film. The first is to change tempos, where a slight slowing down or speeding up can sync point A and B. The second is to keep the same tempo but change the time signature. Taking a beat off or adding a beat or two while trying to keep the music sounding "natural" is a big challenge. Finally, a composer can stop the rhythm in what is called "suspending the time," where the music stops and the instruments crescendo to fill in the exact time needed for the next hit point when they can resume playing.

Danny Elfman describes the difficulty in matching musical tempo to film hit points:

> But when you're in tempo, and you've got 4/4 or 3/4 going, and you've got a tune that's happening, and suddenly, you just can't make it hit anymore. That's a desperate problem. You start doing all these tricks that you have to learn over time like, I have to add

an extra beat or I have to make a 4/4, suddenly a 2/4 or 3/4. You're trying to disguise these cuts in your melody to sound natural. So I started learning many, many years ago, I've got my tune, but I have to add two beats, make it a little crescendo and it goes into the next beat of the melody, and try to make it sound like that's how I intended it, even though it's not.[27]

There are also cases where purposefully composing music to not be in sync with the tempo of the visual image can be very effective. In *The Dark Knight* there is an important final confrontation where the Joker informs Batman that two ferries, one carrying prisoners and the other civilians, have been given detonators to one another's ships. The two have until midnight to blow each other up, or the Joker will blow both of them up. While Christopher Nolan originally planned this as a fast-paced action sequence, Zimmer convinced him to use slower music for the scene, explaining:

I understand why Chris wanted to do this as an action scene. You know, the adrenaline is high, et cetera. It's in that place of the movie where you would have an action scene, geographically, that's where the action scene will take place. But by actually making it slower than what was going on the screen, it added far more tension, and it was a bit more elegant to do.[28]

FORM

Film music, which began in Hollywood during the 1930s, was naturally under the heavy influence of classical music, especially opera. Max Steiner himself was a student of the great Austrian composer and conductor Gustav Mahler, and Richard Strauss, one of the most famous composer-conductors of the turn of the century, was Steiner's godfather. All of the early Hollywood film composers, such as Eric Wolfgang Korngold, Dmitri Tiomkin, Miklos Rozsa, Franz Waxman, and Alfred Newman, had first-rate classical conservatory training. This training was necessary because it trained the skill set needed at the time, which was orchestral composition, orchestration, and conducting.

LEITMOTIF

It was natural for these composers, when confronted with the challenges of this new art form, to make use of their classical composition techniques, and the closest model to the film score was the opera. The particular model of opera that interested Steiner and many of the early film composers was the music dramas of Richard Wagner. Wagner developed the technique of leitmotif, where a recurring musical theme becomes associated with a character, place, or idea. Wagner's music dramas are structured like symphonies in which the orchestra follows the actions of the characters using the leitmotifs. This would prove an ideal technique for the early Hollywood film composers to appropriate in the scoring of motion pictures.

Some of the most popular leitmotifs of our time are the themes from the *Star Wars* franchise, such as the original *Star Wars* fanfare, the Force theme, Darth

Vader's march, Luke and Leia's theme, Yoda's theme, and, for the latest install-
ments, themes for Rey, Kylo Ren, and the First Order.

In the words of John Williams:

> I think that the leitmotif practice, which is to say the technique of some kind of
> melodic identification with a character or a place, is basically how film music works.
> Using a leitmotif or melodic identification with a character admits repetition, so that
> you can hear a theme eight or ten times and you will accept it. Why repetition is good
> is because the viewer will see the film only once and he or she will be mainly distracted
> by the visuals. The more stunning they become, the more deaf we become. So we
> aren't engaged aurally then, so the music needs to function in recognition of that fact.
> So simply put, in trying to create melodic identification we could present Darth Vader's
> theme, for example, and whenever we see him or even perhaps, when we don't see
> him and we want to be thinking about him, the orchestra would state this theme.[29]

Another source of popular leitmotifs is *The Lord of the Rings* trilogy. Howard
Shore composed a wide variety of themes not only for the characters of the
trilogy, but for the locations in Middle Earth as well. The characters such as
Gollum, Eowyn, and the Nazgul have recognizable themes, as do the locations
and cultures of the Shire, Rivendell, Isengard, Lothlorien, Rohan, and Mordor.
The ring itself has a leitmotif which is heard when the film begins, as does the
"fellowship", the comradery that forms the basis of the trilogy.

Discussing his leitmotif approach, Howard Shore says:

> So with the themes and motifs, I was just trying to provide clarity to the story for film-
> making purposes, so people would understand Elves from Lothlorien, from Rivendell.
> Then I created some themes that were more used in a movie sense, like the fellowship
> theme, which is a theme that lasts for the entire world of the movie. I knew that I had
> to create some of those for the world of the Shire, so it had more to do with culture.[30]

James Cameron summarizes this same technique from the filmmaker's perspective:

> I think melody is important because it triggers emotions. Once you begin to associate
> those melodies with something that you've seen earlier in the film, when that melody
> recurs, it can either reinforce what you're seeing, or it can play in counterpoint to it.
> That melody might be associated with a character. You hear that melody after that
> character's dead, [and] all of a sudden you're having a response that's emotional. It's
> visceral. It's happening in a part of your mind that's not even fully conscious, but it's
> working on you.[31]

OSTINATO

Not all melodic film music is based on the leitmotif technique. Instead, many scores
use melody and harmony to create a mood for the film that isn't necessarily related
to any specific character or place. Also, many scores aren't necessarily looking to sync
their themes exactly to the timing of the film. As popular music has started finding
its way into the vocabulary of film music, we can see the rise of more repetitive and
rhythmic styles of composing. Referred to as an *ostinato*, this repetitive, minimalistic
type of composing can be seen in many of the scores of Hans Zimmer.

One of the more famous examples of an ostinato in film music is Hans Zimmer's aforementioned piece "Time" from *Inception*. The piece is constructed from a single eight-bar chord pattern that begins with the solo piano. With each successive eight-bar phrase, more instruments are added until the piece climaxes with a massive orchestral texture and electric guitar.

Another excellent Zimmer example is the piece "160 BPM" from the film *Angels and Demons* (2009). In this case, the ostinato is in the 7/8 rhythm of the melodic and rhythmic parts. A very similar approach to ostinato using rhythm can be found in John Williams' "Duel of the Fates" from *Star Wars: Episode I – The Phantom Menace* (1999). Both pieces make extensive use of both melodic and rhythmic ostinatos. In many ways, much of modern film music has been influenced by dance music, where it's an eight or 16-bar phrase that repeats with builds and drops. Most action music since the 1980s is ostinato based, and it continues to be a very common compositional technique.

Danny Elfman discusses the ease of syncing ostinato music to picture, because in ostinato music you are working in small blocks, which can be copied and pasted, as opposed to thematic composition where you need to try to get the melody to fit a change in the film cut:

> In an action cue you tend to be working start-stop, start-stop, start-stop. You're talking about ostinato patterns, rhythmic things, and you find you can just cut them in and make it work. And you'll find that it's a lot of work, but it's not seriously compromising the music. This is the biggest problem with the thematic composition: you've got a tune, and you're playing the tune, and it used to work, but now [the film editors have] cut just enough seconds from [the scene] that nothing you do makes it happen gracefully. And you either invent and go 'Ah, I've done it,' or you end up just sad, going, 'Well this is how people are going to hear it.'[32]

TEXTURE

Many modern film composers rely on texture and timbre to convey the emotional energy of the film rather than traditional melody and harmony. Many contemporary filmmakers are interested in this type of approach such as the music for the Academy Award-winning thriller *Sicario*. As director Denis Villeneuve explains:

> For *Sicario*, I was saying to myself, 'It's strange. I don't hear music.' People saying, 'What kind of music?' I don't hear music, I hear a threat. I hear a sound that I'm feeling coming under the ground.[33]

The *Sicario* score, by composer Jóhann Jóhannsson, is an interesting example of the use of experimental textures to create the sonic landscape of the film, as well as drones, which are long static notes that slowly evolve over time. For his part, Jóhannsson states:

> For me, the drone can be a very complex thing, even though it's only one tone. When it's really well done, it becomes something that's very, very, simple but very, very complex at the same time. It's very much to do with the fundamental frequencies of the

body and of the world around you. I really wanted a visceral effect that affected the body and affected the audience in a very direct way. And [with] *Sicario* you feel it in your body.[34]

These days, composers are also using noise and natural sound to replace musical instruments as the focal point of the score. For her score for the HBO series *Chernobyl* (2019), Icelandic composer Hildur Guðnadóttir describes her process of going to the nuclear power plant in Lithuania where the series was shot, and recording the sounds of the building with a field recorder, then taking those recordings back to her studio:

We went there to record the powerplant and we wrote the score from those recordings. Every single sound in the score is made from those power plant recordings . . . the big solo musician of the score was this door, which just made these incredible sounds, you know, it was a door to a pump room.[35]

What makes today's world of film composition so interesting is the diversity of approaches and conceptions of how music and sound can work in service of the visual image. Many current composers like John Powell, Henry Jackman, Michael Giacchino, and Ramin Djawadi are using time-honored traditional approaches in new ways, while more experimental composers like Mica Levy, Colin Stetson, and Ben Frost are pushing the boundaries of sound and image.

FILM MUSIC ANALYSIS

After this discussion of the language of film music, the reader may be interested in some approaches to the analysis of film music that may be used at home for your own enjoyment or education. I will propose my own method, as well as introduce two other well-known methods of analysis.

SCORE ANALYSIS

I believe that film scores use three basic textures:

1 Melodic – expressing emotion through recognizable themes and harmonies.
2 Rhythmic – building intensity using rhythm.
3 Atmospheric – using a general mood or texture to convey tone.

Most scores will have a combination of all three of these textures. Take a favorite film and look at one or two scenes at a time, trying to identify the three types of texture is an excellent approach to film-music analysis.

An example of how all of these textures interact with one another can be seen in the opening of the film *Gladiator*. The film begins with a very atmospheric texture, as we read the title cards telling us about the Roman Empire and the background of the narrative. Occasional melodies of Armenian duduk and Spanish guitar can also be heard within the texture, alerting us to the exotic nature of where the film is taking place. We then cut to a scene with Maximus walking through a wheat field, his hand extended to feel the stalks of grain. The atmosphere changes to one where the female voice is featured and Maximus is seen reminiscing, presumably about his family and life as a farmer before the war. Once we get the shots of an army preparing for battle, the texture changes to melodic with the introduction of a new theme in the brass. There is a build in the music until the battle begins, and when it does the orchestra explodes with rhythmic intensity, with the tempo speeding up and the addition of percussion. The battle sequence is an excellent example of a rhythmic texture that also contains some recognizable melodies. Most action sequences will contain both rhythmic and melodic elements, each leading the music at different times.

By watching a scene a number of times, you can begin to recognize some of the themes and be able to differentiate the types of textures with greater clarity. It could be interesting to also look at a number of movies by the same composer and see how their style of composing changes or stays consistent from film to film.

MASKING

Now that soundtracks are readily available on YouTube and Spotify, it's easier than ever to listen to the music of our favorite composers while away from the movie. Can we hear the story progressing by only listening to the music alone? The French film theorist Michel Chion suggests two possible ways of analyzing film music. The first method is called *masking*, where one watches the movie with no sound and then listens to the soundtrack without watching the film. Chion explains:

> This gives you the opportunity to hear the sound as it is, and not as the image transforms and disguises it; it also lets you see the image as it is, and not as sound recreates it.[36]

It can be quite illuminating to watch the film without music and then to feel the emotional power that is added once the music returns. The opportunity to listen to soundtracks away from the movie cannot be stressed enough. To watch a film having pre-listened to the soundtrack is an extraordinary way of mapping the development of the film's narrative over time.

FORCED MARRIAGE

Another very interesting way to explore the power of film music is to mute the film audio and listen to music other than the score. Chion calls this *forced marriage*, saying:

> Take a sequence of a film and also gather together a selection of diverse kinds of music that will serve as accompaniment. . . . Changing music over the same image dramatically illustrates the phenomena of added value, synchresis, sound-image association, and so forth. By observing the kinds of music the image 'resists' and the kinds of music cues it yields to, we begin to see the image in all its potential signification and expression. Only afterward should you reveal the film's 'original' sound, its noises, its words, and its music, if any.[37]

Perhaps the most popular and mythical examples of forced marriage is *The Wizard of Oz* and *Dark Side of the Moon* alliance, popularized in the late 1990s. As the legend goes, if you start Pink Floyd's classic album when the MGM Lion roars, it is mysteriously synchronized to the scenes of the movie. There are numerous lyrical coincidences between the movie and the album. For example, the wordless gospel singing on "The Great Gig in the Sky" is almost perfectly matched with the tornado scene, rising as the storm gathers, falling to a lullaby when Dorothy is knocked out by the window, rising again as the house spins up in the sky, then falling again as the house returns to Earth. When the house finally lands, Dorothy opens the door to reveal Munchkinland, while we hear the sound of cash registers and dropping coins in the opening of "Money." Could this be a commentary about the consumer culture? And then there is the clincher: the album's dramatic ending heartbeats sound as Dorothy listens to the Tin Man's empty chest.

It seems highly unlikely that Roger Waters, David Gilmour, and the other Pink Floyd band members watched the Judy Garland film while recording the record at EMI studios. More likely, it is an interesting example of apophenia, which is the tendency to perceive a connection or meaningful patterns between unrelated or random things. In the words of Chion:

> One perception influences the other and transforms it. We never see the same thing when we also hear; we don't hear the same thing when we see as well.

CHAPTER SUMMARY

* The two most important types of music in films are diegetic music, which is any music that comes from the world of the film, like songs the characters listen to, and non-diegetic music, which is the music that only we, the audience, can hear, which is the score.
* The five main components of film music are style, emotion, energy level, timing, and form.
* Music can have an empathetic relationship to the image by being specific to the emotion and mood of the visual image, or it can be anempathetic by being independent of the image and emotion of the film.
* A common technique that composers use is the leitmotif, a recurring musical theme that becomes associated with a character, place, or idea.

NOTES

1 Chion, Michel (1994). *Audio-Vision: Sound on Screen*. Columbia University Press, p. 15.
2 CNN Transcripts (2002, May 15). *Making the Star Wars Music; Interview With John Williams*. https://transcripts.cnn.com/show/lt/date/2002-05-15/segment/15
3 Epicleff Media (2017, January 12). "Heartbeat of Film James Cameron (Bonus Feature) Score: A Film Music Documentary". *YouTube*. https://www.youtube.com/watch?v=e1AKrk8cA8g

4 Masterclass.com "Martin Scorsese Teaches Filmmaking". https://www.masterclass.com/classes/martin-scorsese-teaches-filmmaking
5 GoldDerby (2021, August 10). "Bridgerton Composer Kris Bowers on Writing Simon and Daphne's Optimistic, Loving, Romantic Theme". *YouTube*. https://www.youtube.com/watch?v=SSFrB1TY2Rw
6 Nostalgia Clipse (2020, October 8). "Jerry Goldsmith Interview (1983)". *YouTube*. https://www.youtube.com/watch?v=typk2o3mhC0
7 Burlingame, Jon (2018, September 3). "From 'ET' to 'Star Wars' and Beyond, John Williams Celebrated at Hollywood Bowl". *Variety*. https://variety.com/2018/music/news/john-williams-40th-anniversary-hollywood-bowl-concert-1202925432/
8 Chion, Michel (1994). *Audio-Vision: Sound on Screen*. Columbia University Press, p. 8.
9 *Ibid*.
10 Masterclass.com "Spike Lee Teaches Independent Filmmaking". https://www.masterclass.com/classes/spike-lee-teaches-filmmaking
11 The Jonathan Ross Show (2022, October 23). "How Hans Zimmer Inspired Christopher Nolan's Interstellar Storyline". *YouTube*. https://www.youtube.com/watch?v=Q7DuMlJHHC0
12 Masterclass.com "Hans Zimmer Teaches Filmscoring". https://www.masterclass.com/classes/hans-zimmer-teaches-film-scoring
13 *Score: the Film Music Documentary*. DVD. Directed by Matt Schrader 2017.
14 Pop Disciple (2017, October 6). *Secrets of the Score 008: Charlie Clouser "Hello Zepp" Theme*. https://www.popdisciple.com/secrets-of-the-score/charlie-clouser
15 Film Score Media (2022, February 11). "Star Wars: Music by John Williams 1980 BBC Documentary". *YouTube*. https://www.youtube.com/watch?v=j3C9fOH-lnU
16 Soundtrackfreak69 (2012, April 18). "John Williams Interview – University of Southern California – Part 3". *YouTube*. https://www.youtube.com/watch?v=WQRoAAnYMgk
17 The Upcoming (2018, February 20). "Benjamin Wallfisch Interview on Blade Runner 2049, Vangelis, Hans Zimmer, Johann Johansson at BAFTAs". *YouTube*. https://www.youtube.com/watch?v=CCMFWx0cFJY
18 John Williams Artificial Intelligence Interview (no longer available).
19 Charlotte Patrick (May 26, 2011). "Hans Zimmer on Creating the Sound of the Joker". *YouTube*. https://www.youtube.com/watch?v=HyQBxCeZ9ls
20 Orchestral Tools (2020, April 25). "LA Creatives: Charlie Clouser and Karel Psota Discuss Sampling + Sound Design". *YouTube*. https://www.youtube.com/watch?v=or7QMpGR2jQ
21 *Ibid*.
22 Lawford83 (2008, June 5). "John Williams Talks Film Music With Gene Shalit". *YouTube*. https://www.youtube.com/watch?v=PlwqlHkF870
23 *Score: the Film Music Documentary*. DVD. Directed by Matt Schrader 2017.
24 Masterclass.com "Danny Elfman Teaches Film Scoring". https://www.masterclass.com/classes/danny-elfman-teaches-music-for-film
25 Lawford83 (2008, June 5). "John Williams Talks Film Music With Gene Shalit". *YouTube*. https://www.youtube.com/watch?v=PlwqlHkF870
26 Masterclass.com "Hans Zimmer Teaches Film Scoring". https://www.masterclass.com/classes/hans-zimmer-teaches-film-scoring
27 Masterclass.com "Danny Elfman Teaches Film Scoring". https://www.masterclass.com/classes/danny-elfman-teaches-music-for-film
28 Masterclass.com "Hans Zimmer Teaches Film Scoring". https://www.masterclass.com/classes/hans-zimmer-teaches-film-scoring

29 Weymouthladuk (2019, December 24). "BBC Radio Documentary: John Williams". *YouTube*. https://www.youtube.com/watch?v=PwanBDlS9ag

30 OxfordUnion (2017, December 5). "Howard Shore Full Q&A Oxford Union". *YouTube*. https://www.youtube.com/watch?v=LxX0r_2x0m4

31 *Score: the Film Music Documentary*. DVD. Directed by Matt Schrader 2017.

32 Masterclass.com "Danny Elfman Teaches Film Scoring". https://www.masterclass.com/classes/danny-elfman-teaches-music-for-film

33 "Making Music for Sicario-Johann Johannsson" (unavailable YouTube).

34 *Ibid.*

35 Epicleff Media (2019, May 21). "Score: The Podcast S2E6 Hildur Guonadottir Needs an Outlet for Her Darkness". *YouTube*. https://www.youtube.com/watch?v=0uNgcKYpWPs

36 Chion, Michel (1994). *Audio-Vision: Sound on Screen*. Columbia University Press, p. 187.

37 *Ibid.*, p. 188.

5

THE CREATIVE TEAM

THE TEAM

The collaborative process in filmmaking requires the coordination of large teams of people working in many different departments. We will now look at the various roles needed for the production of a successful musical score. In larger Hollywood features, each of these roles is taken by a separate person, paid specifically for that position. In smaller independent films, it is often the responsibility of the composer to cover multiple, if not all, of these positions.

The music team is comprised of:

- Composer
- Music Editor
- Orchestrator
- Copyist
- Conductor
- Score Mixer
- Composer Assistants

COMPOSER

The film composer is responsible for every aspect of the original music in a film, from the writing to the recording and mixing of the score. They are not only responsible for the creative work of composing, but also the management of the budget and logistics of realizing their creative vision.

The job of the composer includes:

- Maintaining a budget for all aspects of a film's original music.
- Hiring musicians and music-related staff.

DOI: 10.4324/9781003289722-5

- Meeting with the movie's director to "spot" a film in order to identify all places where music should be present.
- Writing and recording demos to audition various themes for the director's consideration and composing cues in sync with the picture to be approved by the director and/or the creative team.
- Managing the recording of the music, either with live performers, or using software instruments controlled by a MIDI keyboard. Lower-budget films may not have funds to hire live performers, in which case the composer may be personally responsible for performing all the music using software instruments.
- Responding to notes from other members of the production team. Most film composers will insist that their notes come exclusively from the director, but in some cases, other team members, particularly producers, may have the privilege of giving direct notes to the composer.
- Executing a final version of the score that addresses all notes and edit requests, and then provides a final, mastered version of the soundtrack.
- In some cases, writing a separate score to accompany the film's trailer.
- Preparing and editing the score for the soundtrack.

Though technology has been a blessing in regard to the ease with which composers can make demos and sketches of their work to show the director, it has added an extra burden in terms of the skill set which is now expected. According to film composer John Powell:

> We're doing extra levels of jobs that never used to be required. . . . You are the composer, the arranger, the orchestrator, the player, the performer, the producer. All of that has to be finished before you even play a cue.[1]

The music budget shapes the type and sound of the score, just as much as it shapes the creative thinking of the director. Film scoring is an interesting balance between commerce and creativity in this regard. Hans Zimmer is a firm believer in original thinking transcending budgetary boundaries:

> A cheap piano sound, eighty-eight keys, it's all there. And at the end of the day, the job is to go and figure out the notes and figure out all these things. I don't accept the fact that you can't create a great Hollywood blockbuster, or whatever the score is, depending on money, or depending on resources, et cetera. Anybody's got access to something that they can go and make a great score with.[2]

MUSIC EDITOR

Part sound editor, part project manager, and part musician, the music editor oversees the artistic, technical, and logistical aspects of composing and implementing music in film and television. Most importantly, the music editor keeps track of the most current edits of the film and either brings this to the composer's attention or adapts or edits the composer's music to fit the new timings. Additionally, they may create new music or sound effects using portions of the composer's original score.

Danny Elfman explains:

The music editor is going to take all the music and look at what it is, and they're going to follow all the cutting [film edits] that come in as the film is progressing. There's going to be dozens and dozens and dozens of changes in every single cue that the music editors got to keep track of. They've got to be obsessive and fastidious to the extreme because they've got to keep track of everything.

With the advent of digital editing for video and music, some music editors have taken a more creative role as a musical collaborator. Some have the freedom to experiment with using the composer's music in other parts of the film as a creative partner, and to create new musical cues out of layers or parts of the composer's original score as a co-composer.

Hans Zimmer sees his music editor as an essential part of his creative team:

I use my music editors in a very creative way, whereby I just sometimes give them pieces of music without telling them what scene it's for, to see what happens. And something that I knew was going to be only a love theme, he suddenly figures out how to shove it over an action scene. When they put it into the wrong scene it becomes much more interesting. It's a constantly evolving process.[3]

Junkie XL, composer of *Mad Max: Fury Road* (2015), *Justice League* (2017), and *Godzilla vs. Kong* (2021), says:

[Music editors] are the kind that you would deliver like five different cues, sixty different layers of stems [separated musical instrument recordings], and they start creating their own pieces of music, and they time stretch, they pitch shift, they put all kinds of effects on them and create like atmospheric drones from string recordings or brass recordings. These people are almost like a composer themselves.[4]

ORCHESTRATOR

Orchestrators create finished written scores based on the sketches of composers. Typically, an orchestrator receives a recording and MIDI file (with music notation) of an approved composer's mockup, which is a computer emulation of the live orchestra. Using these two resources, the orchestrator must determine the intent of the composer's work and how to best convey it to the orchestral musicians through the language of music notation. Common obstacles include simplifying music that is too difficult for live musicians and determining the optimal way to translate the composer's computer recording for live musicians.

While many composers orchestrate their own music, such as Howard Shore on *The Lord of the Rings,* many others prefer to hand off their computer sketches to an orchestrator because of the time constraints created by the need to compose such a vast amount of music in a short amount of time.

Danny Elfman discusses the important role of the orchestrator:

The most obvious association with most composers is the orchestrator. Almost every composer has an orchestrator that they work with, that becomes somebody they turn to fairly regularly. . . . When I look at my big board with all the cues sitting there, and I have forty-eight starts [cues], and I've only done twelve of them. I don't want to spend one more second than I have to on any detail of this piece that can be worked out by my orchestrator because it's small enough that it doesn't involve me. . . . I need an orchestrator, because I can only take my composition so far before I can give it no more time.[5]

Another reason for composers to use orchestrators is that the orchestrator may have more experience with the orchestra than the composer, and can present a different set of creative options as a collaborator. Many modern film composers have backgrounds in contemporary record production and not in classical orchestral composition. In these cases, the orchestrator becomes an essential partner in the translation of the computer score to the live musician at the recording. Junkie XL continues:

Orchestrators are of great value, because they advise you about what would work really well and what wouldn't work really well. . . . So I constantly rely on the expertise of the orchestrator and the conductor to tell me whether I'm making a good choice or a bad choice, and that's how you learn.[6]

COPYIST

The music copyist proofreads and defines individual parts for each of the individual recording musicians based on the full ensemble score given to them by the orchestrator. Once they have the score, the copyist uses specific notation software, such as Sibelius and Finale, which generates printable sheet music to create individual parts for each musician or instrument.

While much of the job relies on specific skills using the software, the copyist must also consider various factors while producing the parts, including the location of page turns and how the music's presentation will affect each musician's experience playing it. It is not uncommon for the orchestrator to also serve as the copyist.

Composer and orchestrator Penka Kouneva, whose credits include orchestrating the *Transformer* movies, adds:

In most cases, the orchestrator has to stick very closely to the MIDI mockup and there is no space for 'adding stuff.' It's a technical profession whose primary focus is to craft beautiful, flawless professional scores for the recording session. It's not embellishing or changing the composition, and it's not 'arranging the MIDI' because the music has already been approved by the composer's bosses. Some orchestrators do make their own parts, but most don't because the time is extremely tight so they turn to a music copyist. The copyist creates the parts, and then proofreads everything. She needs to watch for page turns and that the parts look most legible and pretty. Both she and I have one objective: for the notation to be so clear and obvious so that all potential questions that the musicians have already been answered in the notation.[7]

CONDUCTOR

A film recording session conductor is responsible for ensuring that the orchestra plays well, assisting the recording engineer to obtain a clean take, and assisting the composer and director to achieve their artistic goals. At the beginning of each session, conductors typically discuss tempo, sonic balance, and difficult musical passages with the composer and orchestrator. In addition to understanding the goals of the composer, film conductors must assist orchestral musicians who most likely have never seen the music they are about to perform. This requires an encyclopedic knowledge of individual instruments and a willingness to address any issues that may arise with the players. Conductors are expected to record 12 to 15 minutes of music per three-hour session.

Speaking of his score for *300: Rise of an Empire* (2014), composer Junkie XL continues:

> The guidance of [conductor] Conrad Pope was very important to hear . . . he conducted the score, and he and I talked a lot about how to do certain things. He knows so much about all these instruments in the orchestra and he can explain to the players really well how they should be playing it. Then he will come up with examples from the classic music or from film scores that these guys potentially have played on . . . it's like, that's how you should play it, with this kind of tonguing, with this kind of articulation. It's incredible to tap into the knowledge of a guy like that.[8]

It is also common for the composer to conduct the orchestra themselves. For many composers, it is a way for them to have direct contact with the musicians and ensure that the performance is exactly as they envisioned. In Hollywood's Golden Age, most of the composers would conduct, and that tradition has continued to stay with us through composers like John Williams, Howard Shore, Brian Tyler, and John Debney.

John Williams believes that conducting skill is fundamental to the study of orchestral composition:

> I have always felt that every composer should conduct to some degree, because the hours on the podium will teach you more about what you're writing than all criticism from your teachers, or anybody else. You discover right away that this can be done better by doing X and not Y. The hours on the podium are the best possible lessons about orchestration.[9]

SCORE MIXER

The score mixer is responsible for all technical aspects of the orchestra or ensemble recording, the final score mixing, and the delivery of audio files to the film's final sound mix, which is called the dub stage. The responsibility around recording includes the selection of mics, their placement, the placement of the instruments, how and where things are recorded, and in what format.

During a scoring session, the score mixer will follow the score to ensure the proper balance between the players on the stage. After the recording session, they mix the orchestra recording, which includes editing the audio and finding the best takes. Once the orchestra is mixed, the score mixer acquires all music files from the composer, which may also include other recordings, synthesizers, or sound design elements the composer has created to enhance the score. The score mixer is responsible for mixing the entire score and preparing the audio files for delivery to the film's final sound mixers, who are called re-recording engineers. Junkie XL explains the role of the score mixer:

> On the musical side, once a composer has written a score, the scoring mixer becomes involved in the process. Before a scoring date, the scoring mixer is the liaison between

the composer and the scoring stage crew, making sure that any pre-recorded elements of a score that need to be heard at a scoring session are delivered, and communicating any special requirements for the physical setup of the orchestra or ensemble being recorded. Once the score has been recorded, the scoring mixer can begin working on the numerous tracks into a variety of six-channel mixes.[10]

A typical 50 to 75-minute score will usually take a week to record, then another week to mix, but that time can vary greatly depending on the composer. A score can be delivered to the *dub stage*, or final sound mix, in several ways; sometimes in a single 5.1 surround audio file, but more often in a series of separate elements called *stems*, to provide the re-recording mixers at the final mix with a greater degree of control. This is done because certain instruments or instrumental groups may be conflicting with the sound effects or dialogue, so rather than turn down the volume of the entire score, the re-recording mixer can turn down only that single instrument or group.

Veteran score mixer Alan Meyerson, known for his work on all of Hans Zimmer's films, including *Gladiator*, *Inception*, and *Dune*, sees his role in a very unique way:

> I don't look at my job as a primary creative endeavor, and I have to be creative, but what I'm really working with is someone else's art, so I'm a service provider. I try to glom my creativity off of what the process they're doing is, so I have this bag of tricks, and when I meet Pinar Toprak [composer of *Captain Marvel*] who's looking for certain sounds and stuff, I go and I pull trick 2,349 and 61. I go, 'Well, why don't we try this and do that, that would be very interesting.' Or Kris Bowers, where he wants to do this piano kind of score for *King Richard*, and so I have an idea for a piano sound. Then in the world of mixing, I'm never satisfied.[11]

COMPOSER ASSISTANTS

Composers who work on films, television shows, and video games require a lot of additional labor and support to accomplish their job. Most hire and employ a small team of assistants that work out of their home or professional studios. Oftentimes an aspiring composer themselves, the composer's assistant is a jack-of-all-trades who does whatever is necessary to support the composer, from getting coffee, naming files, and troubleshooting hardware problems, to writing additional music and, in so doing, gaining insight into the composer's process.

Composer's assistants sometimes facilitate the composition and recording process. This might mean notating a passage as the composer plays it, reviewing notated passages as a proofreader, orchestrating from a composer's MIDI sketch, arranging one of the composer's pieces, or performing on a score, running a recording session, or composing additional music which may or may not be based on original themes of the composer.

Hans Zimmer is a great believer in the educational value of being a composer's assistant, saying:

> I was an assistant to the great composer Stanley Myers, and I learned through his mentorship how to become a film composer. I try to do the same now with my studio, with young composers.[12]

Many of Hollywood's most notable film composers were once assistants to Hans Zimmer. That list includes:

- John Powell – *Shrek*, *How to Train your Dragon*, *Solo: A Star Wars Story* (2018).
- Harry Gregson-Williams – *Man on Fire* (2004), *X-Men Origins* (2009), *Mulan* (2020).
- Ramin Djawadi – *Prison Break* (2006), *Game of Thrones* (2012–2019), *Westworld*.
- Junkie XL – *Mad Max: Fury Road*, *Justice League*, *Godzilla vs. Kong*.
- Steve Jablonsky – *Texas Chainsaw Massacre* (2003), *Ender's Game* (2013), the *Transformers* movies (2007–2017).
- Lorne Balfe – *The Lego Batman Movie* (2017), *Mission: Impossible – Fallout* (2018), *Top Gun: Maverick* (2022).
- Henry Jackman – *Captain America: The Winter Soldier* (2013), *Kingsman: The Golden Circle* (2017), *Jumanji: The Next Level* (2019).

Of his time under Zimmer's mentorship, John Powell reflects:

> Hans was different in Hollywood . . . he actually celebrates the fact that he's got a bunch of other people working with him. It gives him perspective on things, it gives him alternate views that he would never have thought of, it gives him a way of carrying on his knowledge to other people. It's an incredible kind of university that doesn't exist anywhere, and I was a huge beneficiary of that.[13]

CHAPTER SUMMARY

- The film composer is responsible for every aspect of the original music in a film, from the writing to the recording and mixing of the score.
- The music editor keeps track of the most current edits of the film and either brings this to the composer's attention, or they may need to adapt the composer's music to fit the new timings.
- Orchestrators create finished written scores based on the sketches of composer.
- The music copyist proofreads and makes individual parts for each of the individual recording musicians based on the full ensemble score given to them by the orchestrator.
- A film recording session conductor is responsible for ensuring that the orchestra plays well, assisting the recording engineer to obtain a clean take, and assisting the composer and director to achieve their artistic goals.
- The score mixer is responsible for all technical aspects of the orchestra or ensemble recording, the final score mixing, and the delivery of audio files to the film's final sound mix, which is called the dub stage.
- The composer's assistant is a jack-of-all-trades who does whatever is necessary to support the composer, from getting coffee, naming files, and hardware problems, to writing additional music, and in so doing, gaining insight into the composer's process.

NOTES

1 Mix With the Masters "John Powell – How to Train Your Dragon Third Date". https://mixwiththemasters.com/

2 Masterclass.com "Hans Zimmer Teaches Film Scoring". https://www.masterclass.com/classes/hans-zimmer-teaches-film-scoring

3 Mix With the Masters "Score Composition with Hans Zimmer". https://mixwiththemasters.com/

4 Junkie XL (2021, May 28). "Music Editors & Film Scores". *YouTube*. https://www.youtube.com/watch?v=efD8Y85K9Yk

5 Masterclass.com "Danny Elfman Teaches Film Scoring". https://www.masterclass.com/classes/danny-elfman-teaches-music-for-film

6 Junkie XL (2017, May 18). "Film Scoring: What Does the Orchestrator Do". *YouTube*. https://www.youtube.com/watch?v=5LJZXUI1nVQ

7 Kenneth Lampl "Penka Kouneva Interview" (not published).

8 Junkie XL (2019, January 5). "How to Build and Action Cue [Studio Time: S3E7]". *YouTube*. https://www.youtube.com/watch?v=KmtiOLA_60k

9 The Kennedy Center (2022, July 30). "In Conversation With John Williams and Deborah Rutter the John Williams 90th Birthday Celebration". *YouTube*. https://www.youtube.com/watch?v=CKQTbpoH-d0

10 SonixScoop (2021, July 15). "Mixing Masterclass: Film Score Mixing & Composing With Tom Holkenborg". *YouTube*. https://www.youtube.com/watch?v=LzjIfv141IU

11 KMD Productions (2022, March 3). "Alan Meyerson Episode 17". *YouTube*. https://www.youtube.com/watch?v=Znaq2xNkROs

12 "Hans Zimmer Interview". *YouTube* (no longer available).

13 Mix With the Masters "John Powell – How to Train Your Dragon Third Date". https://mixwiththemasters.com/

6

THE CREATIVE PROCESS

THE COLLABORATION

Now that we know the team that composers and directors rely on, we can begin looking at the process they engage in to create their creative magic. This collaboration is unique from director to director, from composer to composer, and even from film to film. This chapter outlines some basic guidelines or milestones that can suggest a structure for each unique collaboration.

Hans Zimmer offers an interesting insight into the process from the composer's perspective:

> Making a movie is a complicated human exercise because, basically, you're dealing with only insecure people at their most insecure. Everybody's worried that what they're doing isn't the greatest thing in the world, and quite honestly, it never is. . . . So, in this environment of total insecurity, sometimes it's really hard to say . . . 'We don't need music here. This scene is perfectly fine, the dialogue is sparkling.' The writer is going to think, 'Well, if I could have only had another seven years, I could have written this line better.' The director is thinking, 'If I had had a better actor, it could have been delivered better.' And the actor, of course, is thinking, 'If I had had a decent director, I could have done a better performance.' And then everybody is blaming the cameraman and the sound recordist, because they're feeling insecure about the scene. They're turning to the last man standing, that's the composer, and they're going, 'This scene needs a bit of help.'[1]

INITIAL CONVERSATIONS

The first conversations between directors and composers generally fall into two categories. The first is one in which the director has a specific composer in mind for the project and is either pitching the project to interest the composer or having a casual conversation about the project to gauge the composer's response. The second category is where a number of composers are being interviewed for

DOI: 10.4324/9781003289722-6

the project, and the director will eventually decide on suitability based on the conversation.

First conversations may be about the style and tone of the score, or a discussion of what the film is about, beyond what we immediately see as the audience. The film *It* (2017), directed by Andres Muschietti, is a great example of a horror film that is ultimately a hidden coming-of-age story. The composer of the film, Ben Wallfisch, recounts that first conversation:

> The first conversation was really that this is not a horror score, it's an adventure score. We had this great conversation. It was this amazing kind of love of those '80s adventure scores of John Williams and Alan Silvestri, all my heroes as a kid. We just connected on that, and making the score about the synergy of those kids coming together as a group, and finding strength. Even though, of course, there's moments of terror and horror, it's a very emotional kind of coming of age story.[2]

Many of the initial conversations can also cover specific types of music. *Bridgerton* composer Kris Bowers recalls how important the specific music input from the producers can be:

> [Producer] Chris Van Dusen asked me to write the piano theme and he sent me a handful of Ravel piano pieces that he was really inspired by. And so for me, that really opened up a lane that I hadn't thought of as far as a sound or a period, because I was thinking, either really specific to that period or very, very modern. That just kind of opened up my mind and immediately made complete sense, just because it has this romantic kind of sound to it. This somewhat mysterious, you know, almost magical kind of quality to it that I thought would be really great for this love story between the two of them. So once I found a theme for Simon and Daphne for that piano piece, that really helped unlock the sound for the rest of the show.[3]

Conversations can also have a more esoteric or philosophical dimension. Hans Zimmer discusses his approach to the first conversations:

> If you take Ron Howard, Ridley Scott, Chris Nolan, and Terry Malick, they're directors that work in very different styles, but at the end of the day, we've all come together at the same sort of place. I have to get into his head, and that's part of the process, because what I want to do is, I want to make the movie that he wants to make, that's what I signed on for. I want to have a bit of his vision. So I work really very hard at trying to understand and have conversations about what this movie is about, and of course, the weird thing is that we don't really talk about the movie. We talk about everything else. We're trying to sort of sneak up on the subject. The conversation is one where we're trying to learn from each other and we're trying to learn from the movie. We're trying to get the movie to tell us how to make it.[4]

As mentioned earlier, Christopher Nolan designed a very unique way of having a first conversation with Hans Zimmer about the music to *Interstellar*, explaining:

> I called Hans before I'd even started work on *Interstellar* and proposed a radical new approach to our collaboration. I asked him to give me one day of his time. I'd give him an envelope with one page – a page explaining the fable at the heart of my next project. The page would contain no information as to genre or specifics of plot, merely lay out

the heart of the movie-to-be. Hans would open the envelope, read it, start writing and at the end of the day he'd play me whatever he'd accomplished. That would be the basis of our score.[5]

Though speaking directly about the film is probably more the norm than the Nolan-Zimmer approach, it is important to remember how unique the first conversation can be.

SPOTTING

Once the composer has been hired, they may begin writing music before the film has been shot. If the film has already been shot and edited, then the next step is what is called the *spotting session*. Spotting is a process whereby a composer and director will sit and watch a rough cut of the film in order to decide which scenes will require music and which will not. The spotting session is crucial, as it lets the composer see and feel the mood of the film in person for the first time, so they can begin to compose music that matches the tone of the film. During this process, the composer will take precise timing notes so that they know how long each cue is, where it begins, where it ends, and particular moments during a scene with which music may need to coincide. As Danny Elfman explains:

> Depending on the film, the beginning is officially the spotting session. You sit with the editor, and sometimes the producer, and certainly the director, and you run the film top to bottom. In running the film top to bottom, you find every moment music starts. Music starts here, it runs two minutes and 15 seconds, and it kind of comes out here. I should add that the really important thing about the spotting session is everybody now knows how long the score is. So from the studio standpoint, this is actually a very important moment because they're going to get a number, and that number is going to tell them how many sessions [recording], how big of an orchestra, and there's a huge budgetary process that has to happen.[6]

TEMP MUSIC

It is very common during the film-editing process for the film's editor to put pre-existing music into the film to serve as a guideline for the tempo, mood, or atmosphere the director is looking for in a scene. This is called a *temp track* or *temp music*. A temp track is often made up of pre-existing classical music, popular music, or, most commonly, other film music, and gives the director an opportunity to inform the composer of what kind of score they're imagining. Once the composer has heard the temp track, they will then compose an original score based on one or more of the elements from the temp track.

Directors like Steven Spielberg will not watch an edit of his films without temp music. Film editor Terry Rawlings, who has worked on the films *Alien*, *Chariots of Fire* (1981), and *Blade Runner*, further explains:

> I don't think anybody is closer to the film than the director and the editor will ever be. I mean, we live with this, it's ours, and the thing is, when you're trying to create a temp

score, then you know the mood you want to create, you know what you want to try and say musically. If you get a mood correct, that's the mood I feel [the composer] should go with. They can change the theme, change the orchestration, but keep in mind the mood that we created."

Experimenting with different temp music is also a way for the director to clarify what they are looking for musically before the composer is involved. Ben Burtt, the editor on the original *Star Wars*, recalls the temp music process with George Lucas:

George had picked a few music cues that he had listened to while he was writing the film. It gave him an inspiration for what he wanted to see and hear. He had a few suggestions, then we were trying different music cues as we went along. We decided where there is music and what kind of music there is. The whole idea of doing a temp track was important because if you have music in the early version of the film, it communicates a lot to the composer. It's easier to put in a cue and say, 'This is the direction I want to go,' than it is to explain it with just words.[7]

The temp music can also be important if film executives want to have test screenings before the composer is finished with the original score.

As popular as temp scores are, some directors do not use temp music from other composers during the editing process because they would like their composer to begin the scoring process with a clean slate. Directors like Christopher Nolan and Denis Villeneuve work this way, and they encourage their composers to start working before the film is shot so they can use the composer's prewritten demos as the temp music for the score.

TEMP LOVE

As good a process as the use of temp music is for the editor and director, one of the dangers is that, after viewing the movie countless times with the temp score in place, filmmakers can develop a case of *temp love*. In other words, the director wants something musically so similar to the temp score that any genuinely new music written for the movie is never as good in comparison, and the composer is strongly encouraged to reproduce the music heard in the temp score.

Composer Christopher Young speaks about this from the composer's perspective:

The whole temp thing has changed everything and the smart political thing to say is, 'I'm okay with the temp, how much of it am I supposed to latch on to, and how much of it am I just supposed to absorb the essence of?' Of course, the temp makes the director more comfortable. I have always preferred the opportunity to see the film for the first time without temp so I can go home and, at least for one evening, think about the film without any music and see where my brain is going?[8]

Danny Elfman further comments:

Temp music is the bane of every composer, and that's a huge part of a composer's job. I'm looking at a film for the first time because usually the very first time I see it, it's going to have a temp score. They may have been working on this film for a year before

I got there, and they've been hearing a temp score for close to a year. So what you've got to do is two things: you can do what I might conservatively say 70 percent of the composers today do, and they just do the temp. Take it, you have the exact tempo, you actually map the tempo out of the temp score and you do something else to the same temp, hitting [syncing] things, using a different piece of music, different melody, but you're going to do the same thing. That is bullshit.[9]

If you listen closely to some of our most beloved film scores, you can hear some of the original temp music's influence on the score. The *Star Wars* fanfare echoes Eric Korngold's score to *Kings Row* (1942) and Darth Vader's "Imperial March" is similar to the Gustav Holst piece "Mars," both of which were the original temp tracks to the film. Part of the genius of a composer like John Williams is that, given the restrictions of the temp score, he created some of the most memorable film music of all time, in many cases even more popular than the pieces they were modeled on.

SUITES AND DEMOS

At some point in the process, the composer must begin writing music. This can happen in the form of a demo, which demonstrates the composer's skill and ability to move from a conversation with the director to actual musical sounds. Oftentimes, composers will create demos in order to be hired, and in other cases, the demo is the way to initiate the first feedback from the director once the composer has already been hired.

Until the 1990s, which marked the advent of digital film-editing systems, the norm was that composers waited until the film was completely edited, which is called a *locked cut*, before beginning to compose directly to the picture. In the modern, fast-paced world of digital editing, composers often write a suite of music based on the script, storyboards, or conversations with the director before the film is shot, or during the edit. These demo pieces can be used in the editing process as the temp music, and in this way the score can evolve alongside the edit. This is the preferred process of collaboration for Hans Zimmer and Christopher Nolan, the latter of whom states:

In each successive film I've done with Hans, I've tried to involve him at an earlier and earlier stage. Adding music to a film doesn't work for me – it's the reason I can't temp a movie. To me the music has to be a fundamental ingredient, not a condiment to be sprinkled on the finished meal.[10]

Christopher Nolan's editor, Lee Smith, elaborates:

Hans comes on early and records just ideas and suites, and kind of anything that comes into his mind through conversations with Chris. And then we start to use that against the images, and very quickly you start to see what will work.

For his part, Zimmer is all for skipping the spotting session altogether:

So now the way I work is, forget the spotting session. Let's just start, if I have the space and the time available. I start when they start shooting and I start off that conversation. I start collecting sounds, and I start making sounds, and I start coming up with ideas, and I start coming up with tunes. Once they're finished shooting, I'm sort of just working in parallel with the cutting room. . . . The old way of writing a score, where you wait for a locked picture, a defined cut, and spend those last six to twelve weeks writing the movie, then going on to a scoring stage, I just don't think that method applies anymore. So it makes sense to try and get some of the work done ahead of those twelve weeks, just so you and they have something to work from when you do need to sit down and think about the score with the picture. You'll probably have more influence over the picture's style and it solves some of those pesky temp score problems.[11]

Thanks in part to Zimmer's success, bringing composers in early in the process to create demos and suites, and using that music during editing for temp score, is now becoming more common, especially in Hollywood.

CUE MOCKUP

Whether a composer is creating demo pieces before the film shoots, or the film is locked and they are scoring directly to the picture, the composer needs to reproduce what the score will eventually sound like before the recording sessions. The entire score needs to be approved by the director before it is recorded, and the MIDI mockup is the way composers simulate the sounds of the score before recording.

A *MIDI mockup* is an extensive demo of a project built using virtual instrument software or hardware to stand in for real instruments. It allows the director or producer to hear the compositions in a setting that approximates their final version, allowing them to approve or alter the project before the budget has been committed to recording live musicians. With the development of faster computers and better software environments for sampling and MIDI editing, most MIDI mockups today are done with software synthesizers and samplers. The replication of acoustic instruments has progressed steadily, to the point where MIDI mockups are occasionally utilized in the final score on films when time has run out or due to budget constraints. According to Danny Elfman:

In this day and age, the directors really do expect to hear a fully rendered piece. Being able to use the synthesizers and the samples does allow me a great freedom to try out ideas. Not only does it allow me to experiment with the composition, but a lot with the orchestration. [Virtual instruments] have been enormously helpful to me in the composition, the orchestration and in achieving the final sound of the demos. These demos are what a director signs off on to get the score done."[12]

Composer Brian Tyler (*The Expendables* (2010), *The Fast and the Furious* (2001)) explains the process of using computer instruments for the mock ups and then replacing the computer instruments with the live orchestra for the final mix:

I tend to write my mock ups. I'll record a sampled version of the orchestra, be it strings, horns, percussion, and all these types of things, and then I'll go and in this case, we went to Abbey Road, and I conducted the orchestra there and it ended up replacing the music of the samples.[13]

FEEDBACK

A crucial part of the role of the composer is the ability to take feedback from the director. Directors have a wide variety of ways of communicating about the music, from specific musical terminology to visual images, colors, or feelings and emotions. It is the role of the composer to be able to decipher the language of the director and translate it into the language of music. As discussed earlier, the use of temp music is a way to bridge that gap. Regardless of how music is discussed, feedback is an essential part of the collaborative process. Disagreement is common, and oftentimes the composer must go along with the will of the director, even if they disagree. For instance, composer Jerry Goldsmith admits to disagreeing with Ridley Scott's ideas in the opening to the film *Alien*:

> I thought, 'Well, let me play the whole opening very romantically and very lyrically, and then let the shock come as the story evolves.' In other words, don't give it away in the main title. So I wrote this very nice main title: it was this sort of mystery, but it was lyrical mystery. It didn't go over too well. Ridley and I had major disagreements over that. So then I subsequently wrote a new main title, which was the obvious thing, weird and strange, and which everybody loved and I didn't love.[14]

Given the nature of continual feedback, rewriting cues is a constant process, and the main part of the composer's job. The translation from the director's vision to sound is especially difficult because it is one of the only parts of the filmmaking process that the director generally has no training in. Screenplay writing, cinematography, lighting, and working with actors are all part of the director's education, but music is not.

Oftentimes, directors may not have a preconceived idea for the score and use the rewriting process of the music to discover the tone of the score. Given the pressures of how fast the score needs to be written and the financial return-on-investment expected from a good score, the rewriting process can be very difficult on the psychology of a composer. James Newton Howard (*Pretty Woman* (1990), *The Sixth Sense* (1999), *Fantastic Beasts and Where to Find Them* (2016)) describes the difficulty of rejection and rewriting:

> Writing is easy. Rewriting is what you end up doing in the film music world. Once you've had a piece of music rejected four or five times from the director, it's very easy to go down the slippery slope of trying to just make the director happy, and it's sort of selling your soul to the devil. It takes a lot of patience to navigate that. I found that I was reluctant to rewrite. I was asking myself, 'Why did I want to strangle a director for not liking a piece of music?' And I realized that part of it came down to just the physical challenge of getting yourself up again, and emotionally as excited the second, the third, the fourth time around that you were the first time.[15]

Many directors also enjoy the feedback and point of view of the composer. Often, a composer may suggest an approach to a scene that the director hadn't considered. Hans Zimmer recalls such an example from *The Dark Knight*:

> I remember Chris [Nolan] being very worried about a certain scene in *Dark Knight*. He kept bringing it up, saying, 'This has to play like an action scene, it has to be fast,

it's got to be really fast music,' and I looked at it and I thought, 'No it's going to be the slowest music I've ever written.' So I wrote this piece at 25 beats per minute, or something ridiculous. I got everybody into the room. I said, 'Chris, I tried something completely different. If you don't like it, I'll just bin it and we'll try the other thing, but I think this could be interesting.' Everybody knew that he'd been going on about this has to be at the fast piece and I played it to him. There was sort of a silence afterwards. He's looking at the screen, and he looks at me, and he goes, 'Oh, yeah, that works, too.' And that was the end of that conversation.[16]

Directors work in many different ways, and part of the role of the composer is to be a type of translator and psychologist in order to understand the director's vision and find a strategy to execute it musically. Once all of the cues are approved, the computer score gets orchestrated in preparation for the recording session.

ORCHESTRATION

Once all of the music has been approved by the director and the recording sessions are scheduled, it is given to the orchestrator, who takes the composer's MIDI mockups and puts what the computer was playing back into notes on a page for the live musicians to read in the orchestra recording session. *The Walking Dead* (2010) composer Bear McCreary explains:

Once cues get approved, then they move into another track of production where it's orchestration and copying. My orchestrators take my MIDI mockups with very detailed markers and they translate my computer notation and my verbal notes into scores, into the music that is put out on the stands [for the recording musician].[17]

Ultimately, the orchestrator's role is to emulate what the cue sounded like from the computer to the live orchestra, the reason being that the director has signed off on the computer-generated cue, and any deviation from that sound could be problematic. As score mixer Alan Meyerson states:

There are many composers today, such as Zimmer and Steve Jablonsky, who do almost all of the conventional orchestration in the computer and create a complete orchestral mockup, which provides the orchestrator with the interesting job of duplicating the mock-up with the live orchestra.[18]

RECORDING

There are a number of ways the orchestra can be recorded, depending on the size, budget, and style of the score. The traditional approach is to record the entire orchestra in one large room. This is how John Williams' scores are recorded. The advantage of this approach is that there is a more natural blend of instruments because every microphone picks up all the instruments. All of the volume balances of instrumental groups need to take place at the time of the recording because everyone is being recorded together. In this way, the recording is of a total orchestral performance, like a live concert. As John Williams puts it:

The recording process is still that process where we want to capture a moment in time, and the moment, or the number of minutes, is a performance. It's good, bad, or indifferent, and that's something that the machines and the computers and the synthesizers won't give to us. . . . The magic of live performance is that we never do the same thing exactly the same twice. I think if we capture a great performance by orchestra and by cast, and put it on the soundtrack of a film, the audience is experiencing something that's organic and alive, and not synthesized and not manufactured by machines.[19]

A second approach, which is more common today because of digital recording, is to record each of the orchestral groups – strings, brass, woodwinds, percussion – individually. This requires a larger budget because of the additional recording time, but the advantage is that the score mixer has more control over the balance (volume) of each group in the final mix. This is especially advantageous if the score is composed of non-orchestral music, like synthesizers or ambient sound design. This is how most of Hans Zimmer's scores are recorded.

Outside of the large orchestral recording sessions, it is also common to have smaller recording sessions for solo instruments or percussion. All of the recordings are compiled by the score mixer into the final mix. Composer Brian Tyler explains:

You have to record them separately only because . . . if you record them in the same room . . . then you don't have any control mix-wise. [Otherwise] you end up with bleeding [unintended sound pick up], so you say, 'Oh, I want the voice louder,' but then there's someone playing the snare drum really loud, and so you try to turn up one thing and then end up both turning up really loud.[20]

SCORE MIXING

Once the music has been recorded, all of the orchestra recordings and composer's audio files go to the score mixer, who compiles them into the final music score. The score mixer will balance the volume of the various orchestral groups with other musical elements, such as electronics, sound design, and samples. It is also common for the sampled instruments and orchestra from the MIDI mockup to be included as a layer in the final score mix. Zimmer states:

I'm not a purist. I use samples, I use synthesizers, I use fuzz boxes, et cetera. I don't write concert music, I write film music, and it's a different thing. We use whatever tools are available to go and tell the story in the way that we can. I mix samples with real orchestra. Sometimes it's just real orchestra, sometimes it's just samples. One of the things about having good samples, and having programmed them well, is it's like a safety blanket for the orchestra. They know if there's a wrong note, I can fix it with the samples, and they can just be a little bit more daring in their performance.[21]

The score mixer is the record producer of the film-music world, and that is why many score mixers, like Alan Meyerson, were, at one-time, pop-record producers. This is how Meyerson sees his role in the process:

In modern film scoring, because the composers tend to be so computer-based, they really have a pretty good idea of what they're trying to get across. So a lot of times what my job is, is to take what they've already done, and add that 5 percent. You know, add that sense of dimension or size or sound that takes it to the next level, that makes it feel polished, or a little bit more emotional, or a little larger than life. And that's really become one of the big jobs I have now.[22]

Once the score is mixed, the score mixer sends the stems, which are groupings of instruments, to the re-recording engineer for the final sound mix called the dub stage. Some common stem groupings are: short strings, long strings, high brass, low brass, orchestral percussion, ethnic percussion, choir, soloists, and synthesizers. The score mixer can make anywhere between ten and 100 sets of stems for the re-recording engineer. In this way, the re-recording engineer has the flexibility to balance each orchestral stem against the sound effects and dialogue of the film.

DUB STAGE

A dubbing stage is a studio facility that looks like the combination of a movie theater and the engineering room of a recording studio, where the final sound mix of the film will be done by the re-recording mixers. The re-recording mixer takes all the previously recorded and edited audio elements – the completed work of production sound teams, dialogue editors, foley artists, sound effects editors, composers, music editors, and music supervisors – and layers them together, balancing the levels. This is where the final decisions are executed with regard to the sonic elements of the film, and it occurs in a theater-like environment to give the decision-makers the best possible representation of how all the elements, audio and visual, are really working together in the context of how the film will be seen and heard.

The score mixer will divide the score into audio files that contain instrumental groups or stems, so that the re-recording mixer has access to the volumes of specific instruments in the music mix. In a certain scene, we may not need the low percussion of the score because of the explosion sounds in the foley. The re-recording engineer needs the ability to take away only that instrument or instrumental group. Similarly, the scene may need a boost in the violin melody because of the loud helicopter sounds from the foley. Again, the volume of the individual violin stems can be raised without raising the level of the entire music mix. Bear McCreary explains:

> Once I sign off on the music, it's printed into mix stems, meaning the strings are separate from the brass percussion, soloists, guitars, high percussion, low percussion, pitched percussion, small percussion, big percussion, synth percussion. The reason that I do this is that on the dub stage, I fully expect to get notes. I expect my clients are going to want to be able to change things and, they should, because when they hear it all for the first time, with the sound effects, the dialogue, edited ADR, the visual effects, they're gonna have comments on the music. . . . So if they say, 'That little drum thing, I don't like that, I want to get rid of that,' okay, let's try it. Then they hear it, 'Oh, yeah, that's much better.' If that track wasn't split out, I wouldn't be able to do that.[23]

The dub stage can also be a very interesting time for the re-recording engineer to get creative with the music in surround sound, by having different parts of the orchestra playing from different speakers, or giving the music depth by having some elements playing from the front of the theater and other elements from the back.

Composers may or may not attend the final sound mix at the dub stage depending on scheduling and the wishes of the filmmaker. Some filmmakers prefer the solitude of making decisions themselves while others encourage points of view from other members of the team. Once the final sound mix is finished, post-production on the film has ended.

CHAPTER SUMMARY

- Spotting is a process whereby a composer and director will sit and watch a rough cut of the film in order to decide which scenes will require music and which will not.
- A temp track is often made up of pre-existing classical music, popular music, or, most commonly, other film music, and gives the director an opportunity to inform the composer in what mood, style, or tempo they would like the score to be in.
- A MIDI mockup is an extensive demo of a project built using virtual instrument software to stand in for real instruments which allows the director or producer to hear the compositions in a setting that approximates their final version, allowing them to approve or alter the project before the budget has been committed to record live musicians.
- Once all of the music has been approved by the director and the recording sessions are scheduled, it is given to the orchestrator, who takes the composer's MIDI mockups and puts what the computer was playing back into notes on a page for the live musicians to read in the orchestra recording session.
- The score mixer will balance the volume of the various orchestral groups with other musical elements and prepares the music mix for the dub stage, or final sound mix.

NOTES

1 Masterclass.com "Hans Zimmer Teaches Filmscoring". https://www.masterclass.com/classes/hans-zimmer-teaches-film-scoring
2 The Upcoming (2018, February 20). "Benjamin Wallfisch Interview on Blade Runner 2049, Vangelis, Hans Zimmer, Johann Johansson at BAFTAs". *YouTube*. https://www.youtube.com/watch?v=CCMFWx0cFJY
3 GoldDerby (2021, August 10). "Bridgerton Composer Kris Bowers on Writing Simon and Daphne's Optimistic, Loving, Romantic Theme". *YouTube*. https://www.youtube.com/watch?v=SSFrB1TY2Rw
4 Masterclass.com "Hans Zimmer Teaches Filmscoring". https://www.masterclass.com/classes/hans-zimmer-teaches-film-scoring
5 Messier, Philippe-Aubert "Nolan on Zimmer, or the New Gospel of Film Music". *Bopper Blog*. https://www.boppermusic.com/blog/zimmer-on-interstellar-or-the-new-gospel-of-film-music/#:~:text=To%20this%20end%2C%20I%20called,heart%20of%20my%20next%20project

6 Masterclass.com "Danny Elfman Teaches Film Scoring". https://www.masterclass.com/classes/danny-elfman-teaches-music-for-film

7 Eicke, Stephan "Of Vaders and Raiders, Interview With Ben Burtt on Film Music and Sound Design". *Media Sound.* https://mediasoundhamburg.de/en/of-vaders-and-raiders/

8 Epicleff Media (2018, May 18). "Behind the Score: Temp Music Score the Podcast". *YouTube.* https://www.youtube.com/watch?v=49TqnDtfP6Y

9 Masterclass.com "Danny Elfman Teaches Film Scoring". https://www.masterclass.com/classes/danny-elfman-teaches-music-for-film

10 Messier, Philippe-Aubert "Nolan on Zimmer, or the New Gospel of Film Music". *Bopper Blog.* https://www.boppermusic.com/blog/zimmer-on-interstellar-or-the-new-gospel-of-film-music/#:~:text=To%20this%20end%2C%20I%20called,heart%20of%20my%20next%20project

11 Masterclass.com "Hans Zimmer Teaches Filmscoring". https://www.masterclass.com/classes/hans-zimmer-teaches-film-scoring

12 Masterclass.com "Danny Elfman Teaches Film Scoring". https://www.masterclass.com/classes/danny-elfman-teaches-music-for-film

13 *Score: The Film Music Documentary.* DVD. Directed by Matt Schrader 2017.

14 Alderete, Andrew P (2011, April 27). "Jerry Goldsmith's Score to 'Alien'". *YouTube.* https://www.youtube.com/watch?v=U8bv0QDLI7M

15 Epicleff Media (2021, September 9). "Score: The Podcast S4E10 James Newton Howard Says Be Great at Making a Demo". *YouTube.* https://www.youtube.com/watch?v=PuhihoyqDuM

16 Masterclass.com "Hans Zimmer Teaches Filmscoring". https://www.masterclass.com/classes/hans-zimmer-teaches-film-scoring

17 *Score: The Film Music Documentary.* DVD. Directed by Matt Schrader 2017.

18 Kunkes, Michael (2009, November 1). "Score Keepers: Mixers Who Capture Composers' Cues". *CineMontage.* https://cinemontage.org/score-keepers-mixers-capture-composers-cues/

19 Stefancos (2007, August 19). "John Williams Talks the Phantom Menace Part III". *YouTube.* https://www.youtube.com/watch?v=lUZmf68rzU8

20 *Score: The Film Music Documentary.* DVD. Directed by Matt Schrader 2017.

21 Mix With the Masters "Score Composition with Hans Zimmer". https://mixwiththemasters.com/

22 Spitfire Audio (2013, November 13). "Spitfire Interviews & Features: Alan Meyerson". *YouTube.* https://www.youtube.com/watch?v=8qI-U6l3N58

23 *Score: the Film Music Documentary.* DVD. Directed by Matt Schrader 2017.

7

TECHNOLOGY AND CREATIVITY

INTRODUCTION

When we think about technology, we think about it as a tool that we use to alter the world around us or accomplish tasks in ways we couldn't without it. It serves a function, a purpose. It is an extension of our own nervous system, allowing us to expand our own biological capacities from information storage and data processing to the manipulation of the physical world. From the invention of the first keyboards, tuning systems, and valved brass instruments, to the development of the electric guitar, synthesizer, and digital recording systems, technological innovations have not only pushed music to explore new creative horizons, but have also shaped the way composers think about writing music.

It was the invention of equal temperament, a keyboard tuning system that first gave pianists the ability to play in all 12 keys, that fostered Johann Sebastian Bach to compose the "Well-Tempered Clavier," a set of 24 preludes and fugues in all 12 major and minor keys. Similarly, the invention of the drumset and the saxophone opened up the avenue to jazz, while the electric guitar opened the gateway for the electric blues, rock and roll, and heavy metal. Technology has advanced not only in the creation of new instruments, but also in the ways that sound is recorded and manipulated. Just as there would be no Beatles without the invention of multitrack recording, there would be no epic *Star Wars* franchise and score without the innovation of Dolby Stereo.

For the savvy composer, it is important to see technological advancements as potential musical instruments. It's easy for us to recognize the electric guitar and the synthesizer as musical instruments because they look and function like traditional acoustic instruments. Though it is much more difficult to conceive of the

DOI: 10.4324/9781003289722-7

computer or a piece of software like a sampler as an instrument, Hans Zimmer observes, as noted earlier:

> You have to start off by realizing that a computer is a musical instrument that needs just as much practice as when you practice piano or the violin or the cello, or whatever. You have to become fairly virtuosic at programming. If you asked me honestly, what my instrument is, I will tell you, it's the computer.[1]

The three important technological innovations that have most shaped modern film scoring are the digital audio workstation (DAW), the synthesizer, and the sampler. Each has influenced not only the sound palette from which composers paint their film scores, but also the process of how composers create.

THE DAW

The biggest technological revolution for both film and music came with the advent of digital technology during the 1980s. Before this time, film was shot on film stock and music was recorded onto reel-to-reel analog tape. Digital technology allowed both the visual image and sound to be recorded or transferred, and then edited as computer data. This freed film editors and music producers from the constraints of needing to cut and assemble film stock or analog tape by hand when creating film edits or music tracks. The *digital audio workstation* (DAW) was an important software developed for the editing of music on a computer.

A digital audio workstation is a software application used for recording, editing, and producing audio files. It is a host application that runs other software. The type of software that DAWs host are called plugins, and they range from virtual instruments, like synthesizers and samplers, to effects for manipulating audio like EQ, reverb, and compression. The most common DAWS for film scoring are Logic, Cubase, and Pro Tools. The DAW revolutionized the way composers worked and for the first time allowed composers to:

- compose music and play it back on the computer, using software to emulate the sound of live instruments prior to the actual recording.
- sync the video to the music so that the score can be composed directly to the movie and all playback is in real-time with the film, allowing for directors to give feedback on the music during the composition process.
- manipulate and transform sound captured as audio recording, and to create new software instruments.
- enter the film-music industry from backgrounds in music production and technology without conservatory training and a prerequisite need to read music.

The ways that directors and composers work together on films changed radically with the advent of the DAW. As previously outlined, the traditional approach to filmmaking was one whereby the director shot and edited the film into a final version called a locked cut. Only then would the director and composer spot the film, discussing at what point the score would begin and end, and what kind of music it should be. The composer would then return to their studio for the next two to three months and compose the score. In some cases, the director would visit the composer's studio to hear some of the orchestra themes played on the piano, but for the most part, the director and composer would not meet again until the orchestra recording session. It wasn't until the recording session that the director would hear the music for the first time. Steven Spielberg comments on using his antiquated process with John Williams:

> John watches the movie and he goes back to his house and he sits alone with a yellow pad and a pencil, and his 100-year-old Steinway piano, and he begins to write the violins, play these notes exactly this time, and exactly at this tempo. The flutes do this, the brass plays here, then the percussion comes in over there. And some of these orchestrations are as complex as Debussy and as accomplished as Stravinsky. But at last he hands this gigantic mathematical puzzle to an orchestra of nearly 100 people [for the recording session].[2]

John Williams continues:

> And then I go off to my studio and write the music, which can take a matter of two or even three months as these films have two and a half hours of music. And then what typically happens is that we meet again on the soundstage and he hears the music for the first time with the orchestra.[3]

Given that the director was hearing the score for the first time, the recording sessions were used to both record the music and to make revisions to the score based on the director's feedback. Sometimes, revisions were made directly by the composer on the spot, or their music team would need to make changes during the recording breaks and have new parts ready for the musicians overnight. In either case, all the revisions were made with the orchestra present, which was very expensive and inefficient.

With the invention of the DAW, composers could create an orchestral mockup, which is an approximation of what the score will sound like using software instruments to imitate the sound of live musicians before the recording. Using this technology, the director has the ability to listen to and approve the entire score prior to the orchestra recording session. Once the recording date arrives, the filmmaker already has a very good idea of what the music will sound like, and revisions at the session are much less likely.

The ability to create an orchestral mockup using a DAW was not only game-changing for the director. It also allowed the composer the ability to compose directly to the picture in real-time, which was not previously possible. Instead, earlier film composers would watch the film on a Moviola, or later on a VHS tape, gather their musical impressions, then go to the piano and start composing away from the film. The composers would write the music on the piano, then with pencil onto manuscript paper, before using a stopwatch and timing codes, translating the film time code into notation on sheet music. In other words, the sync between the music and film lived in the composer's imagination until the final orchestral recording, when the music was played with the images from the film. Prior to the recording session, the composer could only play piano to the film in their studio with rough timing accuracy, and there was never a time for them to sit down and listen to their music play over the film without having to perform it themselves.

The ability to be able to play back the entire score on the computer before the actual recording also blurred the role of the composer and the performer. When composing at the piano and handwriting a score, the score becomes an instruction manual for the performers who record. But when writing at the computer, the composer becomes the performer as well, because they are inputting and adjusting each and every note themselves. As Hans Zimmer describes, the composer creates a convincing performance through his skills in programming:

> When you write on paper, you're basically writing an instruction manual for other people to perform. When you're writing in the computer, the way I do, you perform every note at one point or the other. Every note that is in the score has been played by me and been fiddled around with by me, so it takes a lot longer. Technology doesn't make things faster, it makes it slower because it opens up endless possibilities. Plus, you have to learn how to deal with it so it doesn't drive you.[4]

With the ease of recording directly into the computer, composers now have the opportunity to experiment with manipulating and creating new sounds for their scores. This ability to create new sounds broadened the sonic palate that composers have access to, allowing them to develop unique sounds for their projects beyond traditional instruments. Many of our most beloved modern composers have created unique sound worlds for their scores, which is part of how we identify their compositional voices.

Junkie XL comments:

> Then when digital recording started . . . that's the moment for me, where I started building insane libraries with all the sounds that I made. So for me to make a blend between the organic world and the programming world is . . . taking things that are played by the orchestra, but then treating them with sound design plugins. So whatever the violins are playing, usually is covered somewhere in the sound design world with something else. What the basses are playing is somewhere covered in the sound design world. What the horns are playing is somewhere covered in the sound design world. You create this sound spectrum that . . . makes it more integrated.[5]

As film composition shifted from piano, pen, and paper to the computer, the skillset that the industry demanded of the composer also changed. As music notation and piano skills became less important in the compositional stages, the DAW opened the door for a new kind of film composer: the recording artist and producer, as opposed to the classically trained composer.

Both the computer and the orchestra demand a very specific kind of musical education. From Max Steiner's score to *King Kong* to John Williams' *Return of the Jedi* (1983), the prerequisite for entrance into the world of professional film scoring was a traditional, conservatory-style training. This training was necessary because all of the scores needed to be composed on the piano, written out by hand, orchestrated, and recorded by the studio orchestras. Nearly all of the great film composers from 1930 to the mid-1980s – such as Eric Korngold, Nino Rota, Bernard Herrmann, Jerry Goldsmith, Maurice Jarre, Ennio Morricone, and James Horner – had backgrounds in classical music.

It wasn't until the advent of computer DAW, MIDI, synthesizers, and samplers that the profession of film scoring would open up to composers with backgrounds in record producing and popular songwriting. Composers with backgrounds in popular music – such as Hans Zimmer (The Buggles), Danny Elfman (Oingo Boingo), Mark Mothersbough (Devo), Trevor Rabin (Yes), Trent Reznor (Nine Inch Nails), Cliff Martinez (Red Hot Chilli Peppers), and Jonny Greenwood (Radiohead) – demonstrated the importance of having a virtuosic skill at sound creation and manipulation through their expertise in the use of music technology.

As the computer took a position as the fundamental piece of hardware for the modern film composer, the need for artists skilled in creating music on the computer followed. Ironically, instead of the computer replacing the need for the modern orchestra, it has opened up the opportunity for composers from more diverse backgrounds to use and record with it. In Hollywood, there is more new orchestral music being written now than at any other period in time. Rather than making live orchestral musicians obsolete, the computer has ignited a new interest in orchestral composition.

THE SYNTHESIZER

A synthesizer is an electronic musical instrument, typically operated by a keyboard, that electronically generates and modifies sound. Composers may use synthesizers in the form of physical hardware that features a keyboard and knobs, or the synthesizer may run as software in the composer's DAW. Having first shaped much of the popular music of the 1970s and 1980s, the synthesizer has found an important place in the sound arsenal of most contemporary film composers. Many film scores feature synthesizers prominently, ranging from the early synth scores like *A Clockwork Orange, Halloween, Blade Runner,* and *The Terminator* (1984), to more modern examples such as *Requiem for a Dream* (2000), *The Dark Knight, The Social Network, Drive* (2011), and *Ex Machina.*

There are many reasons that film composers use synthesizers, including:

- to create new sounds and to experiment with new sonic possibilities.
- to produce hybrid scores, which combine electronics with the orchestra or other acoustic instruments.
- to serve as an economical option for film soundtracks when the music budget is too small to hire musicians.

Synthesizers, first and foremost, give composers the opportunity to create sounds beyond what can be produced by acoustic instruments. It is important to note that synthesizers are not primarily used to emulate orchestral instruments but to create original sounds that are not otherwise possible. There are many different types of synths, such as additive, subtractive, wavetable, FM, modular, and granular, which all share a similar signal path. Unlike an acoustic instrument, the signal path of a synthesizer allows composers to control all of the musical parameters individually. The typical signal path begins with the selection of an oscillator or sound source, which passes through a filter to shape the tone with EQ. This tone is then sent to an amplifier, which controls the level of the signal over time before it goes to various effects such as reverb, delay, filtering, distortion, and compression.

Many scores rely primarily, or even exclusively, on synthesized sound. Synthesizer pioneer Vangelis, who scored *Blade Runner* and *Chariots of Fire*, states of the instrument:

> You can go beyond any sound that any conventionalism can produce, without saying that all the acoustic instruments are not valid. I think they're perfect and I think they're always going to be there. But if you want to go beyond that, like, for example, using a microscope or a telescope, then you use a synthesizer.[6]

Hans Zimmer adds that:

> There's an enormous amount of sounds you can discover. I truly think that there are a lot of things that nobody's ever heard because we haven't made them yet.[7]

Synthesizers also increase the opportunities for composers to blend the sound of electronics with that of the orchestra to create a hybrid score like that of Hans Zimmers's work on *The Dark Knight* trilogy and *Inception*. In each of these scores, Zimmer creates specific synthesizer sounds that are unique to those films. Composer John Powell comments on Zimmer's hybrid score:

> If you think of a big electronic score, that would be *Chariots of Fire*, it's a big sound. It's basically electronics sounding like an orchestra, but with an obviously clear synthesized basis. Whereas what Hans has done on *Dark Knight* is blur this line between this giant symphonic sound and electronics, and you're not quite sure where one ends and the other begins.[8]

Many composers use electronics in the background of the score mix to enhance the theatrical sound quality and emotional impact of the orchestra. This is why you may have noticed that orchestral film scores in the movie theater do not sound like classical orchestral concerts. The synths are often hidden in the mix and give an added weight and depth to the orchestra that is not possible with acoustic instruments alone. The electronic elements are felt, but not heard. Composer Alexandre Desplat (*The Grand Budapest Hotel*, *The Shape of Water*) explains:

> I always use electronics in my scores, except they are kind of hidden. You can't really tell. I love playing with my keyboards and looking for sounds, but I like sounds that, whether they're very specific and you can hear them come to the foreground, or they're really all interwoven with the orchestra. In many scores that I've done, there was a lot of electronic and it was mixed with the orchestra. It's something I think that works beautifully if you use the right sound and it's made with taste. I love doing that.[9]

Popular for their ability to sound both traditional and modern, hybrid scores that blend electronic and orchestral elements are very common for action films because of the percussive role the synthesizer can play, with pulsing bass lines and arpeggiated leads. Some notable hybrid scores include the *Marvel*, *Transformers*, and *Matrix* franchises, as well as Ludwig Göransson's scores for *Black Panther* (2018) and *Tenet* (2020).

Music budgets have a lot of bearing on the type of score that is composed for a film. The advent of the synth was a new way for composers to score films on a limited budget without the need to pay recording musicians. A rare example of a director who also composes his own scores, John Carpenter used a synthesizer to write the iconic music to the original *Halloween* because he had no money to pay anyone else to do it. He went on to score most of his subsequent films, including *The Fog* (1980), *Escape From New York* (1981), and *They Live* (1988). Carpenter states:

> You don't have money to hire people to do things, so you have to do it yourself. I started doing music for that reason, because I was half-ass good. I had minimal chops, so I wasn't anything great, but I could at least fake my way through it.[10]

John Powell's primarily electronic and percussive score to *The Bourne Identity* (2002) was due to the lack of budget for an orchestral recording. Powell further addresses the relationship between budget and artistic choice:

> Having electronics is often about the fact that we can't afford an orchestra, or we don't want it to sound orchestral, and that's a deliberate thing, or can we have a bit of orchestra, but make it a bit more hip. So anywhere along that sort of sliding scale of how to make something that everybody expects, but just a little different, or a little cheaper.[11]

The impact of synthesizers on film music has also influenced the way composers think about using the orchestra. Electronic music tends to be more timbre and texture based, and it is not uncommon for composers to ask orchestras to emulate electronic textures with their acoustic instruments. Hans Zimmer speaks about the music in *Inception:*

> We took things which were created completely electronically, these ambiances, these atmospheric tracks, and put them in front of the orchestra and said, 'Okay, now I want the orchestra to go and imitate synthesized electronic sounds.'[12]

THE SAMPLER

As influential as the synthesizer was in popular music, the sampler was more revolutionary for the film composer. Part creative tool and part orchestral place-holder, the sampler had a profound effect on how composers could work on films because it allows them to both emulate live musicians and create new instruments and sounds.

Originally existing as a hardware box, but now operating as software within a DAW, a sampler is an electronic or digital musical instrument that uses sound recordings, or *samples*, of real instrumental sounds that can be performed using a keyboard or computer. The result is an electronic replacement of the instrument being sampled. A sampler does not synthesize the sound of an acoustic instrument because it is a recording of the actual instrument, note for note.

The main difference between a synthesizer and a sampler is that the synthesizer generates its sound from an electronic oscillator as opposed to a sampler which triggers a recorded sample to play. Samplers do not create their own sounds, but playback individually pre-recorded sounds. A sampled piano, for example, is created by first recording all of the 88 notes of an acoustic piano. Those 88 individual recordings are then assigned to their corresponding notes on a keyboard. The keyboard is connected to the sampler, and when the middle C note is pressed on your keyboard, for example, the sampler is playing back a recording of the real middle C (the sample) as performed and recorded on a piano. In this way, samplers are a much better choice when you're trying to recreate real-world acoustic instruments on a computer.

Film composers use samplers to accurately emulate any acoustic instrument, including an orchestra, and to create and manipulate sounds from recordings and perform them as instruments. It is the sampler running from the DAW that allowed composers to create the orchestral mockups that were previously discussed. The sampler only contains the sound of the individual instruments, and it is the DAW that allows you to play back multiple tracks of samplers to create the effect of a large ensemble.

At this point in the book, it should be no surprise that the composer who was at the forefront of sampling, and who created some of the first sample libraries, was Hans Zimmer. Zimmer was the first to attempt to recreate the orchestral recording in his studio using samplers for orchestral mockups prior to the actual orchestral recording session. Oftentimes, the mockups and demos were so good that the directors did not feel the need to attend the orchestra recording sessions at all. Composer John Powell recalls:

> Before Hans, you would write on paper, and you would maybe do a few little bits of demos, you would play things on the piano. But once Hans came along, he basically has the samples that nobody else had at the time because he made his own. So directors often now don't come to the recording sessions because they don't need to. They've heard the cues, all the work has been done . . .[13]

The use of samplers changed the way composers worked on music because, before the sampler, the director did not hear the final score until the orchestra recording session. This meant that any revisions to the score took place during the recording session, which was very stressful and time-consuming. Recalling the old way of doing things, Zimmer comments:

> The idea that you could go and make a sound on the spot, or that you could write a score in an office, as opposed to the whole idea that you had to write it on paper, you have to give it to the orchestrator, and then the first time the director would really hear it would be with the full orchestra there. And he'd go, 'I don't really like this.' And then everybody would go crazy because they'd send the orchestra home and it would be a complete rewrite, so everything was like a compromise and, at the same time, a heart attack.[14]

In Zimmer's view, the value of the sampler was not to replace the orchestra but to enable the director to hear the music before the orchestra recording. In the early days of sampling, orchestras were very hesitant to be sampled because of the fear of being replaced. The opposite has actually taken place, and through Zimmer's pioneering work with sampling, the orchestra is still in high demand for film scores. In Zimmer's words:

> I've been doing this for a very long time, since sampling was invented, and managed to get directors to feel the intention of the music behind the mockup, which is what it's all about, right? I mean, you're supposed to go and let them know what the piece of music is about, what the emotional intent is, but it wasn't about making the music sound better, or making it easier to get the job. It was because I didn't want to sit there all day long, listening to shit sounds. I wanted to spend all day listening to slightly better sounds and I wanted to listen to my favorite players. One of the things I did back then was, because sampling was seen by the orchestra as sort of the enemy, I went to all my favorite musicians in London. I said, 'Look, here's the experiment I'm going to try. If you let me sample you, I will make it so that directors will want more orchestral music, and you will actually get more work out of it because I'm going to be able to present something where they go, "Wow, orchestra is cool, right?"' Because there was actually a time where orchestra was thought of as not cool and it's pretty much actually worked out better than that.[15]

Zimmer continues:

> Hollywood, it has a gazillion bad things you can say about it and they're 100 percent true, but I tell you what, here's one thing it does really well: every day it commissions orchestral music. So that makes me happy because it means that there is actually an outlet for people who want to compose orchestral music. And secondly, it keeps the orchestras alive. So we have just evolved, it's not the Court of Weimar that keeps the orchestra alive, it's now Hollywood.[16]

For his part, Howard Shore associates the use of the sampler mockup to the technique of storyboarding in film production.

> I think of the mockups as you can think of them like storyboards. It's like a pencil sketch of the scene. So they really were just for demonstration purposes. It was a way to have a conversation with Peter [Jackson] about the music, and how themes were used in the film, and how scenes developed, and how the pacing of the film felt. So it wasn't the sound of what we eventually achieved in the recording with the London Philharmonic, but it was a way to work and to have discussions and spotting and things like that.[17]

The birth of the sampler marked the end of the piano, pencil, and paper composer, which had been the only approach to film scoring since the Golden Age of Hollywood. Music editor Dan Carlin speaks on John Williams being the last to compose by hand:

> John Williams is the only composer I know who still only uses a piano, manuscript paper, and a bunch of pencils, and who doesn't have to deliver a mockup. He can get by with that because he is working with one of the most brilliant filmmakers of our time, Steven Spielberg, who is also a major film score aficionado. I don't know of any

other directors who will settle for anything less than a highly refined mockup of the score before it is recorded.

The second, very important, use of samplers is for the manipulation of sound to create complex textures that can be played like an instrument. Each individual sound can be assigned to an individual key, like in the example of a sampled piano, where the recording of the note C4 is assigned to the note C4 on the sampler keyboard. This is called a *one-shot*. But the sampler can also time and pitch stretch the sample. That single audio recording of the piano note C4 can be mapped to the entire keyboard, so when the key C5 is struck, the sample sounds one octave higher and plays twice as fast, or the note C3 causes the sample to be played one octave lower and twice as slow. Keyboard mapping can become very creative when sounds are played at three, four, or five octaves away from the original pitch of the sample. A high violin harmonic when played five octaves lower could become a menacing bass drone. This pitch and time-stretching capability of a sampler allows composers to explore the sonic world beyond the original sampled recording.

This world of sonic exploration can increase exponentially when non-music sounds are used as the sound source of the sampler. An interesting example of this is explained by Charlie Clouser, who used a recording of a screeching subway in New York City to create an ominous string sound for his work on the TV show *Numbers* (2005–2010). Clouser explains:

> One of my most used sounds on the TV series *Numbers* . . . is a sample that I made on a cassette Walkman in 1982, the first time I visited New York City, and I was in the subway and when the subway trains were pulling into the station. Their screeching brakes echoing in the subway station to me sounded amazing. So I recorded the sound of that. I mapped them to the keyboard because they had a definite pitch to them. But when played lower on the keyboard, it becomes very scary. Almost a string section type of sound evolves and goes through changes that were built into it from the act of the subway train squealing its brakes. So the longer you hold down the notes, the more you hear of this evolving sound. And again, it started out with just the screeching little sound, and that was one of the first field recordings that I ever made.[18]

Clouser continues with the importance that samples play during a studio demonstration video:

> Most of the stuff in my template [DAW] here is all samples. That is actually a sample of guitar, its normal pitch is somewhere around here, but when played way down here, three or four octaves below that, it becomes a really evil, girthy, dark sound. And that's something I do a lot of, is taking sounds which have a certain character when played at their normal pitch but then pitching them way down. The sound gets slower as it gets lower in pitch. Most of the things in my working palette are samples and are just being played in the normal EXS 24 sampler.[19]

Using the sampler to create sounds and textures is a way for composers to not only experiment and expand their sonic vocabulary, but also a way for them to create an individual voice as an artist through the sounds they create. Many composers today create their own sounds, and those sounds become the way that we recognize their unique artistic voice. The sonic vocabulary of film composition ranges from traditional thematic scoring to sound design, and the sampler is a tool that effectively blends the world of acoustic instruments with the world of sound design. Using samplers is an integral part of the creative sound design of composers like Junkie XL, who states:

> The orchestral recordings that I make, I treat them with sound design programs, and then add layers of them to the original recording or replace them altogether. So I spent really a lot of time there, and I feel this has become an extra side of my composing career. It gives me a style, it gives me an edge, and it gives me a sound to the overall score.[20]

Composers have always looked for new and innovative ways to make sound. From the innovations of the harpsichord and valve brass instruments like the saxophone, to the electric guitar, synthesizer, or sampler, the evolution of instruments has led to new ways of making music. The pursuit of making electronics as expressive as traditional acoustic instruments has been the goal of many modern composers, including Hans Zimmer, who muses:

> Isn't it slightly annoying that a piece of wood with four strings is still more expressive than all these computers that we've got lying around? So I'm just trying to figure out how I can be as expressive as a violinist with electronics.

COMPOSITIONAL STYLE

One aspect of film scoring that is interesting is the concept of artistic style. A solo artist has the freedom to write and create any kind of music they like, guided only by their inner muse. A film composer's muse, on the other hand, must serve the vision of the director. They do not have the freedom to do exactly as they like artistically, because their music must get approved by the director and filmmaking team. So do film composers consider themselves artists, craftsmen, technicians, or some kind of combination? The following are quotes by film composers addressing the issues of style, craft, and creativity.

Hans Zimmer on the evolving artistic voice:

> There's a certain style that everybody has. Let's call it a voice, and I don't know if one is born with it, one goes into it, or whatever. And then at the same time, things change. I can't imagine writing a *Gladiator* score again, out of no other reason than I said everything I could say on that subject then, and I tried to do it as well as I possibly could. So you lose a little interest in writing Wagnerian heroic themes or something like that, but there's certain chord changes, the way I finished a phrase, it's just me. There's just this little fragment, it's like my signature. Do painters get criticized for painting the same still life the same way, or do filmmakers get criticized for having the shot? You're always trying to do something new, but at the same time, I don't consciously try to work within my style. That's why I shift my projects so radically. Going from an *Inception* to a Jim Brooks movie is a very conscious choice because it's a bit like having a good sorbet before the fillet starts up.[21]

John Williams on style:

> People asked me if I have a style. I don't really know if I do. I think probably not. In working on film, what I've always tried to do is try to provide the music that would live in that particular film, that belongs to the skeletal structure, the fabric and the atmosphere of that particular film. So in the process of doing 100 or eighty or ninety, I really don't know. I've done a lot of these sort of swirling turns stylistically in an effort not to find my style, or to find my voice, but to accompany the film in the intimate, organically connected way that music for that film seemed, to me, to my ear, to need.[22]

Rachel Portman on craft and creativity:

> You are a craftsman, as a composer, whether you write film music or whether you write music for the concert hall, because your craft is your orchestration, it's all those years of learning. Particularly in film music, it's very important to know that it is a craft. You're serving a film, you're not serving yourself, but there is an enormous amount of original creativity within that. So it's two things and they come together in film music where, in a way, when it works, it's a fantastic alchemy, and so often it doesn't work because it's all craft and no originality or creativity, or it's all creativity but it's not grounded. When I'm writing music for film, there's a moment where I actually need to cross that threshold to where I'm actually in the film, and I'm living and breathing, and I become part of it. And then it just all happens naturally.[23]

James Horner on collaboration and compromise:

> In my writing for film, you work for clients, because after all, I'm writing something, it may be stunning to me, and it may be an absolutely wonderful reaction to the film I'm watching, but you're working for somebody, and you're hired by somebody who may or may not share the same tastes, and frequently doesn't. The whole art of film composition for me has become one of gentle manipulation, not only of an audience, but also gentle manipulation of the employer, the director, to accept ideas that he's never heard before and accept them as his own against an image that he's lived with for quite a long time.[24]

Danny Elfman on applying sound to the director's vision:

> You're talking with directors and listening to directors, because, if you're smart, you're really doing more listening than talking, because you really want to hear what they have to say. They're going to express 'How about this? How about that?' No matter what it sounds like, just be open to what they're saying because when they leave, that's the first thing you're going to be doing, is like, 'How do I apply what they just said to what I'm doing?' It's not an easy thing, you're going to find a way to apply it. Hopefully, if you have your sound, you have something that you feel is you, you're going to try to find how it applies through your sound, and you're not going to be imitative and go, 'They want this, I'm just going to give them that.' You want to try to find a way to make it your own version, but what you're going to play them is still clear to them, acknowledging their thoughts.[25]

Michael Abels discusses musical voice as instinct:

> To be creative, to have a voice, you have to know your own instinct about what makes good music. You never play anything for anyone else before you think it's good, and so

that means you're invested in it and, to some level, because you have to listen to your own voice. You know, there's a voice in your head that goes, 'Well, that sucks,' and you have to turn that voice off. But at the same time, you have to get to something where you can say, 'No, that's good,' in response to that voice. So you do that and you write a piece. You can't, if you don't think you can write music, you're right, there has to be part of you that goes, 'This is good and this works and here's why.' I've told students silence is great, so why should you break the silence? If you don't have an answer to that you should not be writing music, because silence is really good.[26]

Charlie Clouser discussing stylistic changes through the scores of the *Saw* franchise:

A lot of the style changes in my approach to [the *Saw* movies] is a response to the different visual styles of the directors. On a couple of the movies that Darren Bousman directed in the middle chunk of the franchise, there was almost a sort of Neo-Gothic aspect to the way he set the production design and the way some of the traps were designed. The visual kind of elements in some of Darren's movies, made me respond by using a kind of epic swelling, choir-type sounds that I would never use, for instance, in *Spiral* [2021], because those kind of visuals don't occur in this movie. So a lot of what I do is responding to the settings and the places that the action is taking place in the movies.[27]

Jóhann Jóhannsson on developing your artistic voice away from film:

It's really through my albums as a solo artist that filmmakers started to notice me. I worked in theater a lot in Iceland, where I got the chance to write a lot of music over a period of time, which was a great opportunity to develop my style and develop my sound.[28]

Junkie XL on music production as artistry:

Production is very important to me. It adds an extra layer, and it makes it easier for me to define who I am as a composer. If I were to write a piece of music just for piano with nothing else, I'd find it very hard to distance myself as a composer from other composers, because a piano is a piano, and there are a lot of really great piano composers in the past that, harmonically and melodically, were able to set themselves apart so uniquely, but I don't see myself in that field. So for me, sound design, production, and extra layering of sounds to what I'm writing is giving me the depth that sets me apart from potential other composers. So that's why production is really important to me.[29]

Hildur Guðnadóttir on curiosity and the strange places in which inspiration hits:

I think curiosity is really my biggest drive. You know, that's kind of why I do music, is because it's out of curiosity, because I spend a lot of time also building instruments. I love writing music when I'm outside, walking or biking or whatever. Somehow it's like the movement of tones are connected to that I'm actually moving in and I'm physically moving, and then whistling something, or humming something, and it'll just kind of hit me, then, if there's something in it. This one main theme of this one film that I'm working on, I wrote it on my bike, and then I recorded it in the dairy section of the supermarket."[30]

John Powell on pragmatism and scoring his first big movie:

I was hired, not because they knew me, or they liked my music, but because Hans [Zimmer] said, 'I can't do this film, but this kid might be able to do it.' So when you're in that position, you're not going to stand there and go, 'I know you want Hans Zimmer. I'm going to give you something completely different that you've never heard before, and it's just going to be amazing.' Given that this is the first big movie I've done, I should probably try and give them what they'd like, what they are hoping for as well as I can, but my own voice is going to come out. So I took a pragmatic approach. I didn't get into film because of my love of film, I got into film because of my love of making music and trying to pay the bills. So it's a pragmatic art.[31]

Hans Zimmer on the challenge of composing:

That's the job, you sit there in front of the piano and there are eighty-eight notes on that keyboard, of which only eleven mean something before they repeat in the octave. And everybody else has played those notes before, and somehow you have to figure out how to write something original with it, but at the same time, not too original, because it has to be appropriate to the story.[32]

CHAPTER SUMMARY

- A digital audio workstation (DAW) is a software application used for recording, editing and producing audio files.
- A synthesizer is an electronic musical instrument, typically operated by a keyboard, that electronically generates and modifies sound.
- Samplers do not create their own sounds, but playback pre-recorded sounds individually.
- The DAW and the sampler changed the way composers write music because for the first time the director could hear the score and give feedback before it was recorded.

NOTES

1 Mix With the Masters (2021, August 27). "Hans Zimmer's Use of Computers and Samples in Orchestral Music". *YouTube*. https://www.youtube.com/watch?v=_LHyNYRtwR8
2 McCarthy, James (2019, November 13). "The Art of Film Music". *Gramophone*. https://www.gramophone.co.uk/features/article/the-art-of-film-music
3 Karthik Nagarajan (2007, July 20). "John Williams With LSO for SW2-AOTC". *YouTube*. https://www.youtube.com/watch?v=PRWOudms6sk
4 Salvor Seldon (2021, August 2). "The Sound and Music of the Dark Knight Rises, a Behind the Scenes Look". *YouTube*. https://www.youtube.com/watch?v=xnIasa7n6bI
5 Orchestral Tools (2019, March 13). "Tom Holkenborg: Sound Design in Film Music". *YouTube*. https://www.youtube.com/watch?v=U172Nhiayxg
6 Andreasrocky (2007, December 15). "Vangelis-The Man and His Music (Part 2)". *YouTube*. https://www.youtube.com/watch?v=6Usoz20gXKo
7 Moog Music Inc. (2015, October 15). "Hans & Clint Masters at Work". *YouTube*. https://www.youtube.com/watch?v=NdG5dEfAcxQ
8 *Score: The Film Music Documentary*. DVD. Directed by Matt Schrader 2017.
9 Film Music Institute (2021, January 28). "Film Music Live With Alexandrew Desplat". *YouTube*. https://www.youtube.com/watch?v=sgcwMp6XBgQ

10 Film.Music.Media (2018, September 22). "Director/Composer Interview: John Carpenter". *YouTube*. https://www.youtube.com/watch?v=1xwjViFY_pM

11 *Score: The Film Music Documentary*. DVD. Directed by Matt Schrader 2017.

12 Elegyscores (2011, March 30). "Hans Zimmer – Making of Inception Soundtrack". *YouTube*. https://www.youtube.com/watch?v=W1FIv7rFbv4

13 Mix With the Masters "John Powell – How to Train Your Dragon Third Date". https://mixwiththemasters.com/

14 BAFTA Guru (2018, July 26). "Hans Zimmer on Scoring Gladiator, Inception, Interstellar & More". *YouTube*. https://www.youtube.com/watch?v=D1-eXPXQwzs

15 Mix With the Masters "Score Composition With Hans Zimmer". https://mixwiththemasters.com/

16 *Ibid*.

17 Runar Lundvall (2022, April 30). "How Howard Shore Made His LOTR-Mockups". *YouTube*. https://www.youtube.com/watch?v=CCF0eL1eBmM

18 Pop Disciple (2017, October 6). "Secrets of the Score 008: Charlie Clouser 'Hello Zepp'". *Theme*. https://www.popdisciple.com/secrets-of-the-score/charlie-clouser

19 *Ibid*.

20 Junkie XL (2017, May 4). "Film Scoring: The Importance of Production". *YouTube*. https://www.youtube.com/watch?v=G15uW5Hbq7A

21 "The Best Hans Zimmer Interview Part 2". *YouTube* (not available).

22 Weymouthladuk (2019, December 24). "BBC Radio Documentary: John Williams". *YouTube*. https://www.youtube.com/watch?v=PwanBDlS9ag

23 Lampl, Kenneth "Rachel Portman Interview". Not released.

24 TED Blog Video (2015, January 24). "James Horner's TED Talk on Composing Film Scores". *YouTube*. https://www.youtube.com/watch?v=xIcwsQgQrEg

25 Masterclass.com "Danny Elfman Teaches Film Scoring". https://www.masterclass.com/classes/danny-elfman-teaches-music-for-film

26 Epicleff Media (2019, July 2). "Score: The Podcast S2E12 Michael Abels went from K-12 Classroom to Hollywood". *YouTube*. https://www.youtube.com/watch?v=VbPydLaLXeY

27 Film Music Institute (2021, May 20). "Film Music Live With Charlie Clouser". *YouTube*. https://www.youtube.com/watch?v=I3w9b0uGB4Y

28 "Making Music of Sicario – Johann Johannsson". YouTube (not available)

29 Junkie XL (2017, May 4). "Film Scoring: The Importance of Production". *YouTube*. https://www.youtube.com/watch?v=G15uW5Hbq7A

30 Spitfire Audio (2018, April 9). "Hildur Guonadottir (Joker, Chernobyl, Sicario: Day of the Soldado) Discussing Composing for Film". *YouTube*. https://www.youtube.com/watch?v=5H5a2m-XFD4

31 Film.Music.Media. (2015, September 11). "All Access: John Powell – Episode 1". *YouTube*. https://www.youtube.com/watch?v=-E1bIOvlGuI

32 Hans Zimmer Teaches Film Scoring. www.masterclass.com/classes/hans-zimmer-teaches-film-scoring

8

THE FUTURE OF FILM SCORING

An Introduction to Video Game Music (Co-authored by Thomas Connell)

INTRODUCTION

From the coin-op arcade games of yesterday to the consoles, computers, smart-phones, and VR headsets of today, the video game industry has grown so dramatically since its earliest days that it now makes up the largest slice of the entertainment industry pie. Ever since their inception in the early 1980s, video games have enjoyed an explosive rise in revenue, a growth only strengthened by the COVID-19 pandemic, where home gaming's almost entirely digital marketplace was allowed to flourish, while traditional media, including in-person cinema, saw a crash in profits because of local and national lockdowns. The difference between the two is stark: global video game revenues hit $179.7 billion in 2020, while the film industry only reached the $100 billion mark.

VIDEO GAMES AND FILM

The mediums of film and video games are similar at first glance: they are both a form of on-screen storytelling, yet they are also fundamentally different when one takes a closer look. One key difference is their treatment of linearity. A film will be the same on every playback, with each audience member or viewer seeing and hearing the same plot points, the same characters, the same music, and the same dialogue, delivered in the same order every time. A video game, on the other hand, can be a different experience at each repetition, with no two players ever experiencing a game in the same exact way. Though the overall story arc will remain the same, each player creates their own narrative based on the game choices they make. In this way, gameplay is more similar to the decision-making process of our day-to-day lives.

The role of choice not only differentiates video games from film, but it represents a new way of approaching narrative storytelling. As David Cage, the video

DOI: 10.4324/9781003289722-8

game designer of *Heavy Rain, Beyond: Two Souls*, and *Detroit: Become Human*, explains:

> The way we tell stories has not really changed since Aristotle defined the rules of trag-edy about 2,500 years ago. According to him, the role of storytelling is to mimic life, and make us feel emotions, and that's exactly what storytelling as we know it has done very well since then. But there is a dimension of life that storytelling could never really reproduce: it is the notion of choices. In a play, a novel, or a film, the writer makes all the decisions in advance for the characters, and as the audience we can only watch passively the consequences of his decisions. As a storyteller, I've always been fasci-nated with the idea of recreating this notion of choices in a fiction. My dream was to put the audience in the shoes of the main protagonist, let them make their own deci-sions, and by doing so let them tell their own stories.[1]

Different playthroughs and different players can lead to different choices. Games can reward players by catering to these choices. For example, one player may choose to argue with a non-player character, removing them from their avatar's friend group, whereas another may romance them, unlocking new dialogue and abilities. Video games allow for an interaction with the story, rather than the pas-sive act of merely viewing cinema. That is not to say that cinema is less engaging than video games, just that games require the player's active involvement, while a movie will run from start to end even if no one is watching. In a film, the audi-ence observes and responds to the work of the writer, director, and actor. In this way, the collaboration is between the people making the film and not with the audience. In a game, on the other hand, the player becomes a collaborator in the experience of gameplay. David Cage continues:

> The experience is very unique, because it is the result of the collaboration between a writer creating this narrative landscape and the player making his own decisions tell-ing his own story and becoming the co-writer, the co-actor, and the co-director of the story. Interactive storytelling is a revolution in the way we tell stories.[2]

SIMILARITIES IN VIDEO GAME COMPOSITION AND FILM SCORING

STORYTELLING

In both video games and film, music is used to convey the narrative. Music can help to tell the story of the characters, events, or world, and it can support the visuals on the screen. Music serves to enhance the immersive experience of their respective mediums, setting the tone for different levels and environments in games, which in many ways are analogous to scenes in a film.

Just as it is the film composer's job to capture and enhance the story with music, the same holds true for video game composers. Inon Zur, composer of music for the *Fallout* and *Dragon Age* games, describes the importance of telling the story with music:

> First the story. What is it about? The three big W's: *when, where* and *why*. The *why* is the whole motivation for the story. When you get that, then you know the *when*: Is it in

the past, in the present? Is it in the future? It influences the music. The *where* – sometimes it's an imaginary place, sometimes it's a place that exists – it will be where the actual game happens. *Why* is the most important: what is the story about? What is the motivation? What are all the emotional aspects that are being drawn from the story that could be enhanced by the musical score?[3]

There are many ways to tell the story and many different perspectives to tell it from. *Assassins Creed* composer Jesper Kyd looks to tell the story in a less direct way:

The storyline is the number one thing you think about, and I always try to find things in my music where I can express something that we might not necessarily see or expect when we're playing this moment, because if you're playing a moment, and it has an emotional resonance already, then you don't always have to play into that. That scene might already be emotional enough, and if you put music that's expected in there, it will make it more emotional for sure. But if you can find a way to score something that you don't necessarily see, but you're perhaps scoring the background story a little bit.[4]

LEITMOTIF TECHNIQUE

The use of leitmotif is a very important part of developing the narrative of a story. In film, the technique developed from modeling the compositional process of film scoring on that of the opera. In video games, the technique originated from the initial hardware and data storage constraints of early video games. Due to both hardware limitations and the tiny amount of data storage space on a game cartridge for audio, composers had to reuse some of the sound assets they created. In a ten-hour game, there was not actually enough room to have ten hours of unique background music. As a result, music was one area in which video games turned their early limitations into strengths.

One such way of conserving audio data was the use of leitmotifs, which could be repeated and varied throughout the game. Since early games could only have so many songs, composers wrote a song for each important element of the game. Each character and location had their own theme songs, along with a few songs to indicate specific moods. Now, technically, the term leitmotif is used to refer to the recurrence of a short theme or fragment of a melody that returns throughout the course of a soundtrack. These early games, however, used entire songs in the soundtrack that symbolize a specific narrative element, rather than a short thematic motive more commonly associated with the traditional leitmotif technique found in film and opera.

At the end of the 1980s and all through the 1990s, technological advancements in gaming consoles allowed for an explosion of RPGs (role-playing games). RPGs are famous for having great storytelling, and the music became the perfect tool to enhance the narrative experience. With the increase in storage capacity and the ability to synchronize audio to images in consoles like Nintendo, composers like Nobuo Uematsu (the *Final Fantasy* series) and Koji Kondo (*The Legend of Zelda* series) began using leitmotifs as a standard way to link the soundtrack to the story in a way that paralleled its use in film and opera. This technique can be found today in video games ranging from *Hollow Knight*, *Metal Gear Solid*, and *Call of Duty*, to *Mass Effect* and *Resident Evil*.

This idea of developing strong music themes that can function as leitmotifs is the most important first step in the compositional process, according to *Doom* composer Mick Gordon:

> On any project, whether you're scoring a film or game, the most important thing that you do first is to develop themes. Develop strong melodies, and repeating patterns or motifs. If you've got a strong set of themes, writing an extra half an hour of music is nothing, because you're just expressing that melody in different ways. And if you've got a really well-written melody that works with different chord progressions, it can be extended in different ways, reinterpreted in different ways. Honestly, it's like printing ideas.[5]

In practice, the recurrence of a leitmotif theme becomes a central part of the emotional experience of gameplay when it's recognized by the player. *Halo* composer Marty O'Donnell explains:

> The emotions that the player has when they first experience a piece of music has equity; it's like money in the bank. I know that if I bring some version of that melody back, I'm going to be tickling that emotional bank account that you already have going. Emotions you had the first time, you remember. That makes it easier to compose, because you're like, wait, that was a good theme, I'm going to do a variation on that theme.[6]

CINEMATICS

Video games often contain *cinematics* and *cutscenes*, which are both short, non-interactive movies that play during the game. Cinematics are short in-game CGI movies often used to advance the plot, introduce new characters, provide exposition, or add emotional impact to important moments in the game. Cutscenes are a type of cinematic shown to the player when they reach a particular point in the game, such as at the end of a level where the scene finishes automatically while the player is still in active gameplay mode. Put another way, a cinematic is a self-contained narrative idea, whereas a cutscene continues the action of the gamer while in gameplay mode.

While cinematics and cutscenes are not interactive, they can still be an essential part of the gaming experience, by advancing the story and providing players with a sense of immersion and investment in the game's narrative. As *Bioshock* composer Garry Schyman explains:

> Many games have what are called cutscenes or cinematics that are in fact scenes which are CGI movies that you score just like you would a scene in a film. But there's also the gameplay footage, and the gameplay is what makes game music different from film music, because it's not locked picture, but it is occurring in a certain place and time in the game.[7]

Many games incorporate so many cinematics that they could be considered films themselves. Lorne Balfe describes the music of *Assassin's Creed 3*:

> There was far more cinematics and cutscenes in it, and basically the feeling was to try to get more film-esque with it. I think there was probably about 70 minutes of cinematics alone. It's the length of a film.[8]

COLLABORATION

Both video game and film composers often collaborate with directors, producers, and other creative team members to develop a shared vision for the project's
music. They must be able to communicate effectively with others and work
within a team environment to create a cohesive musical score. In film, composers
most often collaborate and take feedback from the director, and in video games
it is often from an audio director. Composer Garry Schyman explains:

> You have a person, it could be a music director or it could be an audio director, and
> they're giving you direction. They're doing gameplay capture videos, so someone will
> play the game, and they'll capture the video of that gameplay and then that is provided
> to you. Then they'll say, 'Okay, we want a two-minute looping cue to play during this
> portion of the game.'[9]

Given that many video game companies are now the same size as many film
companies, if not larger, the structure of the large video game productions are
very similar to those of major Hollywood films. Composer Austin Wintory
comments:

> Working with a company like Ubisoft, or Sony, or Microsoft, you end up working with
> the audio department in a way that's much more like the old Hollywood days. And you
> don't even interact with, or have only passing interactions with the closest equivalent
> to the Spielberg or whoever that project would be if there even is one.[10]

DIFFERENCES IN VIDEO GAME COMPOSITION
AND FILM SCORING

MIDDLEWARE

In order for the music in a game to be interactive with the gamer's decisions, a
program is needed to mediate this interaction. Middleware is a type of program
that sits between the game engine and the sound files for the game. When a
sound is required by the game engine, a call is created, which is then processed
by the middleware that queues an audio file to be played. Middleware mediates
between the behavior of the player in the environment and the appropriate
sound which that behavior triggers. This mediation can range from new music
being triggered by a player's proximity to a goal or the pace of the music being
moderated by the intensity level of a battle. As the player interacts with the game,
the middleware mediates how the music and sound play in response to their
actions. Wwise and FMOD are two widely used middleware options for the
video game industry.

The implementation of audio through middleware is the responsibility of the
audio department. Implementation refers to the process of integrating audio
assets (music or sound fx) into a game engine or platform. This includes all the
technical aspects of bringing audio into a game, such as programming audio
playback, syncing audio with game events, and optimizing audio performance.
The implementation of audio is a highly creative process that needs to answer

questions like: What triggers the music to play? What triggers it to intensify or subside? When should new music begin or end and how loud or soft should it be? Through middleware, musical triggers can be mapped to anything from the proximity to visual objects, places, and characters in the game, to levels of health or fear. The structure of the implementation becomes the basis of the musical structure.

Composer Jason Graves describes how, in the game *Dead Space*, layers of music are triggered by the level of fear registered on the fear meter, which requires much more music to be written to encompass all gameplay scenarios:

> The idea is the layers of music are being turned up and down based on a fear meter. So maybe you were getting close to him, but you hadn't seen him yet, and the music starts getting louder. Then when you finally see him, a stinger [musical hit] will play and then the combat music starts. But that whole bit of gameplay lasts 15 seconds, so you've got all these layers moving back and forth during 15 seconds of the two-and-a-half-minute loop. A lot of times this two-minute piece that I wrote, that's actually eight minutes of music, will be playing in-game for 20 minutes and you'll never really hear the same thing twice. It doesn't sound like a loop, because it's constantly moving up and down and changing with your gameplay, and on top of that, we have random stingers that play. I did like sixty different stingers and they just randomly will trigger a certain size stinger, or when something happens, so it really keeps it evolving and keeps it from getting stale, which I think keeps it scary as well.[11]

Part of the collaborative process of game composition is not only capturing the right tone and emotion of the story, but to work with the audio team and decide what type of music is triggered by what type of event. This is called audio implementation and is a creative art form in itself. The cooperation between implementation and game music is an important part of the success of the game. Composer Winifred Phillps explains:

> The implementation itself is such a richly creative process. They have a vision, sometimes it's a really grand vision and I don't want to say, 'Look, this isn't in your ballpark, this is in mine, and I'm going to do this.'[12]

Phillps continues by discussing how her involvement in the implementation of audio changes from game to game:

> I was working very closely with the developers at Twisted Pixel and we developed the whole musical system hand-in-hand, and I put together the musical implementation plan for that. I was working with them on where the triggering points would be and it was very collaborative. But there are other teams and other projects in which their vision is guiding me in terms of the way in which they like the musical matrix to come together with all the different musical elements.[13]

IMPORTANCE OF LOOPS AND LAYERS

The challenge of game composition and implementation is how to keep both consistency and interest in the music within a potentially indefinite time of gameplay. The use of layered music loops is one of the most common solutions.

Music loops can be two, four, or eight measures of repetitive musical motifs, which can be layered in order to increase or decrease intensity depending on the implementation strategy. *Tomb Raider* composer Jason Graves describes the process of the interaction of layers:

> There's four different layers of music all playing at the same time. If you're exploring, there's just the bottom layer, and a second layer will come in, and then eventually, all four of them will turn on, but for every two-minute piece of music I wrote, it was actually eight minutes of music. So if we're doing two hours for the score, that means we're actually recording eight hours for the score. In order to do that, I had to record all the sounds beforehand, and then cut them up and put them in the computer and write the music that way. It was very backwards.[14]

The repeating music loops can be varied by having *intros* (beginning section) and *outros* (ending section), as well as musical hits called *stings*. This variation gives the gamer the impression that the score is custom-tailored to their experience. Garry Schyman explains:

> One of the simplest but still most common interactive techniques is just to loop the cues so the cue just keeps playing over and over again. But there are other interactive techniques. The layers can be stingers, or it can be intros and outros, or it can be lots of different ways to make the music feel like it's scoring every player's gaming experience, which is what really makes game music different from film or TV music, which is locked picture.[15]

One of the difficulties with games is that the gameplay time will vary considerably from player to player, and it would be impractical, if not downright impossible, to commission a composer to write enough music to cover every scenario. Commenting on the difficulty of composing such a small amount of music in relationship to the total time of gameplay, Winifred Phillips says:

> Themes are tricky in video games, particularly with looping content, content that's going to be repeated a lot. You can spend hundreds of hours playing a game and there are only a few games that are actually requisitioning hundreds of hours of music. So there's going to be repetition happening there and it's a good point that you have to be very aware of that as an aspect of what you're doing.[16]

FULLY COMPOSED PIECES

One advantage of not composing music to the pre-existing timeline of the film is that the composer can compose without the timing restrictions of the image. This allows the composer to write in a more organic way, by letting the piece unfold naturally without the burden of synchronicity. This method is similar to freely composing concert music or songwriting. Inon Zur relates the process of composing game music to that of classical concert music:

> I believe that writing for games is actually a more pure way of composition, because in many, many cases, you will compose a full piece. When you compose music for film or for TV, you're locked to a picture, and so it cannot really grow and evolve and develop

and start the way the composer will want. But in video games, it's totally different. The in-game cues . . . are like mini pieces: they have a beginning, introduction, development, recapitulation, and everything. It's almost like the old way of composing music. We're not bounded or limited by the picture.[17]

Garry Schyman adds:

Game music is a little more akin to writing for the concert hall because you don't have any imagery that you're locked to. You have a mood that you're setting, so that's its own unique challenge.[18]

COMPOSITION BEGINS IN PRE-PRODUCTION

In games, the composer is brought in to compose music as the game is being developed, and the composer's original music is tested in the game all along the way. In this way, the composer becomes part of the process of developing the world of the game. For his score to *Flow*, Austin Wintory recalls:

We had a design document that was literally just printed out of Word and then prototypes of the game. Music drafts were written at every step, so it's not like the film process of delineating into pre-production, production, and post-production. Especially on a game like that, where the score is half the experience because it's the entire audio, it was just a lot of wild experimentation, and a lot of things not working."[19]

In film, it is still common for a composer to be hired in post-production, once the picture is locked, and after temp music has been used in the editing. In games, the audio directors often look to explore a variety of musical possibilities with the composer, which parallels the development of the game rather than relying on temp music. Garry Schyman comments:

[Video game music is] different from film and TV to some extent. They sometimes know what they want, they have a sense of it, but very often they don't. A lot of film and TV will have temped their score and they just want you to emulate it. But in games they haven't put in any temp music, and they tend to hire you earlier in the process. They don't really have a strong direction.[20]

WORKLOAD

In film, a composer is generally given six weeks to three months to compose between 30 and 120 minutes of music, depending on the length of the film. Game composers are usually brought in at the development stage of the game and thus have from six months to two years to compose from three to six hours of music. Composer Austin Wintory describes the difference:

I've certainly done quite a few indie films, and am accustomed to the four to eight-week turnaround. I think the shortest I've ever done a large-scale project on a game was, like *Assassin's Creed* was 10 months or something. That was over three hours of score. But even still, you could do like 10 movies in 10 months.[21]

Lorne Balfe has composed film scores for *Top Gun: Maverick*, and *Mission Impossible: Fallout*, as well as video game scores for *Assassin's Creed* and *Call of Duty*. He sees the role of the composer as the same in both mediums, with the difference being one of composing time and the amount of music:

> I've never seen a difference between gaming and filming. I think it's trying to do the same job and the only difference is that I have to write far more music for games than for a film. On a film, you'll average 70 minutes, and on a game most likely three hours, so it's quite a bit more. But you tend to have more time with the game because they're developing it for two, two and a half, three years, so you've got a longer window.[22]

FROM FILM MUSIC TO GAME MUSIC

Many of today's top video game composers began first as film or television composers. In the late 1990s and early 2000s, video game creators were seeking experienced orchestral film and television composers to write for their games, which were becoming increasingly more cinematic. *Fallout* composer Inon Zur began his career as a composer for Fox Family Channel and made soundtracks to the Fox TV series *Digimon* and *Power Rangers* before receiving an interesting call:

> One day, I received a weird phone call and a very gruff and official voice came out of the phone. 'Hello, my name is Bob Rice and I'm representing composers for video games.' And I said, 'Okay, so let's get these things straight, you're representing composers that write music for video games? Okay, I didn't know that there is music in video games. I thought that's always like some electronic sounds. That's it.' And he said, 'No, no, no, no,' and he asked me, 'Would you like to try to compose music for computer games?' And I said, 'No, thank you, not for me. I'm here for the big Hollywood film or TV shows.' But he was very, very stubborn and he asked me, 'Do you like to write for orchestra?' And I said, 'Yeah, that's my dream,' and he said, 'Do you know that in computer games nowadays,' we're talking 1996, 'people are actually recording classical orchestras for computer games?' And he started sending me some scores. And it's like, 'Wow, really? You know what, let me try it.' So we tried, and the first game I did was for Interplay and it was *Star Trek: Klingon Academy*. It was my first game and I recorded the Seattle Symphony and I recorded a choir for it. It was like a dream come true, and since then I was just hooked.[23]

Bear McCreary is known for his work on the television series *Battlestar Galactica* (2003–2009), *The Walking Dead* (2010–2022), and *Agents of S.H.I.E.L.D* (2013–2020), as well as the video games *God of War*, *Call of Duty Vanguard*, and *Godzilla: King of the Monsters*. His video game scoring career began through game developers being fans of his music from *Battlestar Galactica*. McCreary recalls:

> I got involved in games, mainly because game developers and producers have been *Battlestar* [*Galactica*] fans and so it's gotten me into a lot of meetings. I met with Morgan Gray and everybody on *Dark Void*, and we hit it off immediately. I mean, they really responded to this sound that I bring to *Battlestar* and to *Terminator*, and I really responded to the story and the production design and the artwork, which is all that I had to see at that moment. The same year or a year later, I did my first Sony project, which was *SOCOM 4 U.S. Navy SEALs*, and in fact, it was that game that connected

me with the Sony Music Department who brought me in on *God of War*. . . . But in both cases, I was brought in because of this symphonic kind of Hollywood, lyrical, expressive sound that I had applied to *Battlestar Galactica*.²⁴

FROM GAME MUSIC TO FILM MUSIC

There are also a group of composers who began their careers in video game composition before expanding into film scoring. The most notable example is Academy Award winner Michael Giacchino, who has composed scores to: *The Incredibles*, *Up*, *Rogue One: A Star Wars Story* (2016), and *Spider-Man: Homecoming* (2017). Giacchino began his career as a composer for DreamWorks Interactive, composing music for their video game series *Medal of Honor* and *Jurassic Park* under the mentorship of Steven Spielberg.

In 2001, producer-director J.J. Abrams discovered Giacchino through his video game work and asked him to provide the soundtrack for his new TV show, *Alias* (2001–2006). Abrams was specifically interested in Giacchino's ability to bring his orchestral video game soundtrack approach to the series. Giacchino would go on to provide the score for Abrams' 2004 television series *Lost* (2004–2010) and many feature films, such as *Mission: Impossible 3* (2006), *Star Trek* (2009), *Super 8* (2011), and *Star Trek: Into Darkness* (2013).

Speaking on how he discovered Giacchino, J.J. Abrams says:

> I remember when I was playing the *Tomb Raider* video game when that first came out, and the music just had a tone and a feeling that was so transportive. It was as much part of the experience as any of the visuals. It was the first time it hit me how cinematic video games were going to become, and so when I heard the music that you had been doing for *Medal of Honor*, those are amazing scores. I'd created this show *Alias* and I thought, well, I need a composer who's going to give this thing scope and emotion and depth. In TV, typically, it was more of a kind of a guy with a couple of synthesizers and maybe a few session players, but I wanted orchestral score.²⁵

Jesper Kyd is a BAFTA-winning Danish composer who has created music for video game franchises like *Assassin's Creed*, *Borderlands*, *Darksiders*, *Hitman*, and *State of Decay*, which led to his film and television scores for the Chinese box office fantasy action-adventure *Chronicles of the Ghostly Tribe* (2015) and the SyFy TV anthology series *Metal Hurlant Chronicles* (2012–2014). His introduction to the team of the internationally acclaimed dark fantasy film *Tumbbad* (2018) came through his music for the game *Hitman*. As Jesper Kyd explains:

> I was approached by the team. Sohum Shah and Adesh Prasad, and Adesh was a big fan of my music for *Hitman*. He really thought that my music was crazy enough to fit this movie, because when they did show me the movie, I could just immediately tell that this movie was something special. I also realized that this movie is so beautiful, and it has so much atmosphere that it's going to be a challenge to compete with that, and that's when I knew this would be a great project to be a part of.²⁶

DO COMPOSERS NEED TO BE GAMERS?

So, is being a video game player an essential part of composing for games? Some composers sound off:

I was always interested in games. I like playing games; I had Nintendo and Super Nintendo, but it never occurred to me that I would have a career, that there would even be a place for someone that would do real recorded music like that in games. – Mary O'Donnell

(*Halo, Destiny*)[27]

I always loved movies and television and games. In video games, over the course of my childhood, I was the exact age where video games grew up with me. When I was five, games were meant for five-year-olds, when I was 13, games were starting to come out for 13-year-olds, and when I was a teenager, the art form kept evolving. My career started in television and then I started to get to do some video games. – Bear McCreary

(*God of War, Dark Void*)[28]

Once I got the Commodore 64 – which is like the first game console video game and the first computer that actually has an analog sound chip inside – these scores were really incredible back then, I remember getting into video games, and video game music at the same time, playing these games on a Commodore 64 and hearing what these composers could do with this analog sound chip. I had never heard anything like this before, it absolutely fascinated me and that's when it just became completely addicting. I had to do, like, a track every day. – Jesper Kyd

(*Assassins Creed, Hitman*)[29]

People that know me, they know very well that I am not a, what you call a per se gamer. I am enjoying playing games, specifically the games that I actually didn't do, because I love to hear what other people are doing. This is part of the reason why I'm playing; I want to listen to what the other guys are doing. But I'm not a gamer. This is not how I'm spending my free hours. I have a lot of passion for the gaming industry, that's totally different. Even though I'm not a gamer, I know about games more than your most avid gamers will know because I invested myself into getting into the whole inside of making all the soundtrack for games, and in order to do that, I had to understand the whole thing inside including the soul of the gamer. – Inon Zur

(*Fallout, Skyrim*)

Until two and a half years ago, I never knew the world of games, I never played games, I never kind of saw games. So it's been an absolute wonderful eye opener now to kind of get into this world, and now most of next year is booked with games. – Lorne Balfe

(*Assassins Creed, Skylanders*)[30]

I get asked all the time, how important is it that I be a gamer? And I always say, 'Look, I have plenty of composer colleagues that don't play games in their spare time. I do. I love games.' So no, technically you don't have to be a gamer. But if I was a game developer, and I was interviewing composers, and it felt like this person, they're not fluent in the language of the thing I'm trying to build and they don't empathize with or even understand what my problems are. – Austin Wintory

(*Journey, Flow*)[31]

FINAL THOUGHTS

Filmmaking has had a significant influence on many aspects of video games, including storytelling, cinematography, special effects, performance capture, and especially music. The cinematic orchestral style has become even more popular as narrative storytelling has influenced game production. Many composers believe that the newer art form is the next evolutionary step beyond cinema. Hans Zimmer explains:

> As games develop, as this new art form develops, we can become more cinematic, and as we become more cinematic we can actually go and surpass what we have in the cinema. I think that's interesting because one of the reasons I really enjoy the whole gaming world is because we are looking for that next thing, which can become immersive, that can involve us, that can really, in a way, go beyond entertainment.[32]

Austin Wintory asserts that interactive music is nothing short of revolutionary:

> Interactive music is this amazing frontier that I think is going to take its place as an art form in the 21st century, with no precedent. And potentially it could be the dominant form of musical expression of the 21st century because it would be like a reinvention of music itself.[33]

In either case, both cinema and video games are a strong cultural force in modern society, reflecting both our stories and our choices. It will be interesting to see how both evolve in the years to come and what we can understand about ourselves through this evolution.

CHAPTER SUMMARY

- As technology has advanced, video games have become increasingly cinematic in terms of narrative storytelling, visual effects, and orchestral scores.
- The most important difference between film and game scoring is that the composer is not composing to a locked picture but instead with loops and layers, which can accommodate a variety of choices made by the player in the game.
- Middleware is software that mediates between the behavior of the player in the environment and the appropriate sound which that behavior triggers.
- Video games often include cinematics, which are short in-game CGI movies used to advance the plot, introduce new characters, provide exposition, or add emotional impact to important moments in the game.
- Video game composers begin to work while the game is being developed and a score could take one to two years to finish.
- Video game scores can range from three to six hours of music.

NOTES

1 TE (2018, December 13). "How Video Games Turn Players Into Storytellers". *YouTube*. https://www.youtube.com/watch?v=XowcxCYbug0

2 *Ibid*.

3 Soundiron (2019, July 16). "In the Studio – Interview With Inon Zur". *YouTube*. https://www.youtube.com/watch?v=yE9iwOz9ueI

4 Gameumentary (2017, December 15). "Jesper Kyd Documentary – Bound to Sound". *YouTube*. https://www.youtube.com/watch?v=EIlFfHkSgaU

5 Gordon, Mick. Personal Interview.

6 RPGeebz Music Arcade (2022, November 22). "Marty O'Donnell Is Back – The Halo Journey, Never Forget and Supporting Doom Composer Mick Gordon". *YouTube*. https://www.youtube.com/watch?v=OIJashjVy8k

7 Schyman, Garry. Personal Interview.

8 Film.Music.Media (2012, January 17). "FMM: Composer Interview – Lorne Balfe (1/16/2021)". *YouTube*. https://www.youtube.com/watch?v=jsTHNCkcCqo

9 Schyman, Garry. Personal Interview.

10 Film.Music.Media (2017, November 1). "All Access: Austin Wintory". *YouTube*. https://www.youtube.com/watch?v=WMc3LbHQ4U0

11 Pyramind (2019, November 22). "Dead Space Interview w/composer Jason Graves". *YouTube*. https://www.youtube.com/live/NQvV6Z3BOO8?feature=share

12 Ehtonal Canada (2019, October 25). "Winifred Phillips Game Composer Interview". *YouTube*. https://www.youtube.com/watch?v=bhuUtMQIWo0

13 *Ibid*.

14 Pyramind (2019, November 22). "Dead Space Interview w/composer Jason Graves". *YouTube*. https://www.youtube.com/live/NQvV6Z3BOO8?feature=share

15 Schyman, Garry. Personal Interview.

16 Ehtonal Canada (2019, October 25). "Winifred Phillips Game Composer Interview". *YouTube*. https://www.youtube.com/watch?v=bhuUtMQIWo0

17 Film.Music.Media (2015, December 17). "All Access: Inon Zur". *YouTube*. https://www.youtube.com/watch?v=MoaipKCrrqU

18 Schyman, Garry. Personal Interview.

19 Film.Music.Media (2017, November 1). "All Access: Austin Wintory". *YouTube*. https://www.youtube.com/watch?v=WMc3LbHQ4U0

20 Schyman, Garry. Personal Interview.

21 Film.Music.Media. (2017, November 1). "All Access: Austin Wintory". *YouTube*. https://www.youtube.com/watch?v=WMc3LbHQ4U0

22 Film.Music.Media (2012, January 17). "FMM: Composer Interview – Lorne Balfe (1/16/2021)". *YouTube*. https://www.youtube.com/watch?v=jsTHNCkcCqo

23 Film.Music.Media (2015, December 17). "All Access: Inon Zur". *YouTube*. https://www.youtube.com/watch?v=MoaipKCrrqU

24 G4TV.com. (2013, March 3) "gtv.com-video38234: Dark Void Bear BcCreary Interview". *Vimeo*. https://archive.org/details/g4tv.com-video38234

25 Manufacturing Intellect (2016, July 13). "JJ Abrams and Composer Michael Giacchino in Conversation and Q&A (2011)". *YouTube*. https://www.youtube.com/watch?v=VRvQOQ1Xp8U

26 Gaautaam Goswami (2020, April 21). "The Music of Tumbad | Sohum Shah | Jesper Kyd | Aanand L Rai". *YouTube*. https://www.youtube.com/watch?v=bWB_jJujyog

27 IGN (2016, March 25). "Halo and Destiny Composer Mary O'Donnell – IGN Unfiltered Interview". *YouTube*. https://www.youtube.com/watch?v=xwugLKltVqo

28 Rolling Stone (2022, November 5). "God of War Ragnarök Composer Bear McCreary Details His Career & Kratos' Next Chapter | RS Daily Show". *YouTube*. https://www. youtube.com/watch?v=yJgkwf8ZFb4

29 Austin Wintory (2021, April 28). "Stories from a Musical Assassin || Jesper Kyd – Game Maker's Notebook". *YouTube*. https://www.youtube.com/watch?v=qm-I6pS0W0k

30 Film.Music.Media (2012, January 17). "FMM: Composer Interview – Lorne Balfe (1/16/2021)". *YouTube*. https://www.youtube.com/watch?v=jsTHNCkcCqo

31 Akash Thakkar (2020, September 22). "How to Succeed as a Game, Film, and Concert Composer | Interview With Austin Wintory". *YouTube*. https://www.youtube.com/watch?v=dEapCPj6AHI

32 PlayStation Australia (2013, August 23). "Hans Zimmer & Lorne Balfe on composing BEYOND: Two Souls soundtrack". *YouTube*. https://www.youtube.com/watch?v=tYs1e307QSs

33 Akash Thakkar "How to Succeed as a Game, Film, and Concert Composer | Interview With Austin Wintory". *YouTube*. See 22, 2020. https://www.youtube.com/watch?v=dEapCPj6AHI

9

THE FUTURE OF FILM SCORING

The Trilogy, the Series, and the Franchise

THE EXPANSION OF STORYTELLING

As cinema evolved, films became longer. In the early days of cinema, films were only a few minutes long and were shown as part of vaudeville shows or nickelodeons, but as the film industry grew in popularity and sophistication, the length of films increased. By the 1930s, feature-length Hollywood films began to emerge, with run times of 90 to 120 minutes. By the 1960s, some of the first film series emerged, such as the *Godzilla* (1954), *James Bond* (1962), and *the Pink Panther* (1963) franchises. This may have been due to the popularity of the recently developed television series of the day, which drew large audiences but had very low production value due to smaller budgets and technical limitations.

During the 1960s and 1970s, the film trilogy format gained popularity via Sergio Leone's *Dollars Trilogy* and *Star Wars*. The film trilogy was different from the film series, as each film in the trilogy is designed to stand on its own as a complete story while also completing a larger, three-part narrative arc. Due to the popularity of the original *Star Wars* movies, many trilogies followed, such as *Indiana Jones* (1981–1989), *Back to the Future* (1985–1990), *Toy Story* (1995–2010), *The Matrix* (1999–2003), *Lord of the Rings* (2001–2003), the *Bourne* series (2002–2007), and *The Dark Knight* trilogy (2005–2012).

This increasing popularity of the trilogy then gave rise to modern film franchises like the *Marvel Cinematic Universe, Star Wars, Harry Potter, The Fast and the Furious*, and *Mission: Impossible*.

By the mid-2000s the growing popularity of premium cable, followed by streaming services, along with the digital innovations of film, editing and effects, television networks, and streaming services could compete with the film industry in terms of creating content with high production value that could match, and in some ways outdo, the theatrical experience. Introducing this so-called "Golden Age of Television," series like *Alias, Lost,* and *Game of Thrones* gained

DOI: 10.4324/9781003289722-9

increasingly large audiences, and with this popularity, budgets increased to the point that the episodes of many TV series were spending as much money as large theatrical films.

Of course, the film trilogy and franchise, as well as the newfound length and budgets of television series, have led composers to think and work differently.

THE THEATRICAL TRILOGY

The original *Star Wars* trilogy is the first set of three films produced in the *Star Wars* franchise, created by George Lucas. The original *Star Wars* film received widespread acclaim from critics for its storytelling, characters, groundbreaking visual and sound effects, and John Williams' musical score. Both *Star Wars* and *The Empire Strikes Back* have been hailed as among the greatest and most important films of all time, turning fantasy and science fiction films into a blockbuster genre. Beyond that, *Star Wars* became a pop culture phenomenon, spawning a multi-million dollar merchandising empire and a fast-expanding universe of films, series, and amusement parks. Inevitably, the success of *Star Wars* led filmmakers and film production companies to think about the trilogy as a new way to both tell stories and earn profits.

The trilogy format poses a very interesting challenge in the world of composition. Should there be themes or musical motives which link the three films, or do the three films stand as musically independent entities? John Williams describes how his music for the first film in the *Star Wars* prequel trilogy, *The Phantom Menace* (1999), prompted George Lucas to think about how that music could work in the subsequent sequels of the trilogy:

> Suggesting and giving hints of themes that we already know was, for me, a new experience on this *Phantom Menace*. I think it's a thought that probably is going to emerge as being a more important thought as we move on to the next couple of episodes. In the choral piece of *The Phantom Menace*, when George heard it, he said, 'Ah, that's the theme of the last film.' I'm not sure what he means because he has something in his idea that I don't know about. But this musical image seems to kind of connect in his mind with something that's yet to come, so I can imagine in the next episode that we'll be revisiting some of the music already now created for *Phantom Menace*.[1]

Many trilogies use a single composer for the entire series, including John Williams' work on *Star Wars* and *Indiana Jones*, Alan Silvestri on *Back to the Future*, Don Davis on *The Matrix*, Howard Shore on *Lord of the Rings*, Hans Zimmer on *The Dark Knight*, Randy Newman on *Toy Story*, and John Powell on the *Bourne* films.

How difficult is it for composers to work on a set of three films which are interrelated, as opposed to a standalone film? Composers often find the process of scoring three films an invigorating experience. *The Lord of the Rings* composer Howard Shore shares his enthusiasm about working on an entire trilogy:

> I was still very energized, even more than at the beginning, because I had the whole background of the piece behind me, and because *Fellowship of the Ring* was successful, it actually boosted you to take those pieces and create *Two Towers* and *Return of the King*. Also the bar just kept getting higher because you went from *Fellowship* to

Two Towers to *Return of the King*. Each one is actually improving and getting better and becoming even bigger productions.²

In other cases, especially when the project isn't conceived as a multipart series from the start, the composing of the trilogy can be quite challenging in both reworking material from the earlier films and revisiting old material if there are large spans of time between the films. There is also the added challenge of the first film being thought of as a standalone project, as in the case of *Batman Begins* (2005). Hans Zimmer reflects on the difficulty of *The Dark Knight* Trilogy:

> When we did *Batman Begins*, we never thought we would do a sequel, it never occurred to us to do a sequel. We thought we would do one movie. *Batman Begins*, *Dark Knight* and *Dark Knight Rises*, that's twelve years of my life, three movies, to you. But for me coming back to a motif ten years or so later, and I still have to be able to get something out of it, I really dug myself a hole there. You know it became very complicated.³

Some trilogies use different composers for each film such as the *Alien* trilogy (1979–1992) scored by Jerry Goldsmith, James Horner, and Elliot Goldenthal, the *Hannibal Lector* trilogy (1991–2002), scored by Howard Shore, Hans Zimmer, and Danny Elfman, and the *X-Men* trilogy (2000–2006), scored by Michael Kamen, John Ottman, and John Powell. In many cases, where there is a new composer for each installment of the trilogy, no music is shared between the films.

THE FILM FRANCHISE

A film franchise is a collection of related films in succession that share the same fictional universe or are marketed as a series. Many of the most popular trilogies, like *Star Wars* and *The Lord of the Rings*, have evolved from trilogies to become entire franchises. The highest-grossing movie franchises of all time include the *Marvel Cinematic Universe*, *Star Wars*, *Harry Potter*, *Spider-Man*, *James Bond*, *Avengers*, *Batman*, *The Fast and the Furious*, *X-Men*, and *The Lord of the Rings*.

John Williams speaks on the pressure of having to compose for the second *Star Wars* trilogy given the success of the first:

> You and I talking now in 1999, which is over 20 years since the trilogy started, and it's daunting for me or for any composer to start any project. You think, well, will I be able to solve the problems? Will I be able to come up with something as good? Can I hit the ball as far as I did the last time?⁴

Many franchises have a theme that becomes the musical brand of the franchise and that single theme is heard in each film regardless of the composer, such as the iconic themes associated with *Star Wars*, *Harry Potter*, *James Bond*, *Mission: Impossible*, and *Halloween*.

MISSION: IMPOSSIBLE

This single-branding theme written by the original composer of the series can pose unique challenges for the new composers of the franchise. The easily recognizable *Mission: Impossible* theme, composed by Lalo Schifrin for the original TV series in 1966, became the trademark of the series and of all the subsequent films. There have currently been six films in the series (two more on the way as of this writing) and it is interesting to see how different composers have grappled with the use of Schifrin's established theme. Danny Elfman, who scored the first *Mission: Impossible* film in 1996, says:

> Once the decision was made to do the score in an overblown orchestral way, there was no analyzing that. It was always intended, when the theme would be played – and there were two major spots where it did – that it would sound bigger. The feeling was that Lalo [Schifrin] had written it to be played by a small ensemble, and it sounded great on TV, but now we're doing the movie and it's much bigger, and the feel of the theme has to be much bigger.[5]

Michael Giacchino, who has scored two films in the franchise – *Mission: Impossible III* (2006) and *Mission: Impossible – Ghost Protocol* (2011) – remarks on the difficulty of having to limit the number of times the theme is heard:

> The Lalo Schifrin theme is without a doubt one of the greatest themes ever written and so the joy of being able to use that theme in a huge, giant summer movie is one of the greatest gifts you could get. It was also one of those things that you couldn't just play over and over and over. It's the greatest thing in the world, but you can't use it for 90 minutes of music as score. You don't want to because when you're telling a story, you want to save the peak of the story for a very specific time in the film and it's the same with the music, we wanted to be able to just hammer away at that theme at the perfect time.[6]

By the time Joe Kraemer was brought on to score *Mission: Impossible – Rogue Nation* (2015), the film franchise was firmly established, and now there was a legacy of not only the original Lalo Schifrin theme, but the scores of the other composers of the earlier films: Danny Elfman, Hans Zimmer, and Michael Giacchino. Kraemer explains:

> I had sort of gotten a blessing from Tom and the director to not go back and watch the first four *Mission* movies again. I don't want to copy what Danny [Elfman] and Zimmer and Giacchino did. However, the director said, 'Well, that's great, you know, because I don't really want to make a sequel to *Ghost Protocol*, I want to make the biggest episode of *Mission: Impossible* anyone's seen.' So I went back and started watching the first [original television] season again and I saw how Lalo used the plot theme, and how different writers would incorporate elements from the *Mission: Impossible* theme. As I was doing this demo for the airplane sequence, anytime I sort of stepped outside of that sound of the '60s, it started to feel wrong to me. I wanted to be a little more of an homage and less of a pastiche. More of a continuation and less of a sort of wink and nod look back.[7]

Lorne Balfe, composer of *Mission: Impossible – Fallout*, comments on the difficulty of not only having the iconic *Mission: Impossible* theme, but on finding a new approach to the score while remaining consistent with the musical style of the *Mission: Impossible* franchise:

> I knew all of the films musically; from how Danny [Elfman] was the beginning of the film franchise, and then how Hans [Zimmer] twisted it and turned it around, and then

THE FUTURE OF FILM SCORING   115

Michael [Giacchino] and Joe [Kraemer's] interpretations of it. You've got a lot of DNA to work with, but the main thing was to try to give a fresh, different approach, but also be respectful. I think that when you watch it, you have to feel that you're in that *Mission: Impossible* world. The soundtrack to *Fallout* is different than the other movies but the movie alone is different. To me the movie depicts what the score is going to be, so it may not be as classical as the others but it's a different tone this time.[8]

Balfe continues describing how intimidating it was to be part of an iconic franchise:

You've got one of the most memorable themes in the world and it's very intimidating touching something like that. It's intimidating and an honor to be able to play with that melody. You're being invited into this family and it's intimidating because of the legacy that's there. Once you start you have to put that to the side and treat it no differently than anything else which is next to impossible because you're constantly thinking wait a minute this is *Mission: Impossible* and there's Tom Cruise, it's difficult to separate them.[9]

SUPERMAN

Based on the comic-book character first published in 1938, and first adapted into the 1948 television series starring Kirk Alyn and Noel Neill, the *Superman* franchise has been around for quite a long time. The franchise found a resurgence in 1978 with the Richard Donner film starring Christopher Reeve and Margot Kidder. John Williams was the composer for the film, and he created the iconic "Superman March" for which this iteration of the franchise is known. The second reboot took place in 2006 with X-Men director Bryan Singer's *Superman Returns*, featuring a theme composed by Singer's longtime collaborator John Ottman. This film was followed by a series of Zach Synder films, *Man of Steel* (2013), *Batman v Superman* (2016), and *Justice League*, with scores composed by Hans Zimmer and Junkie XL.

Bryan Singer's *Superman Returns* (2006) acts as a continuation of the world created by Richard Donner's *Superman* (1978). Before Singer agreed to direct the movie, he made sure that he could secure the use of John Williams' original theme as a main musical motif. Composer John Ottman recalls the pressure of having to live up to that legacy:

I immediately, without even saying anything, felt this pressure on my shoulders looming, because I know what that meant. I was going to be fed to the lions no matter what I did because I would have to use John Williams' theme. Bryan said in that phone call that he wouldn't have even gone forward with this film if he wasn't sure he could use the Williams theme. . . . I tossed and turned in bed every night and had every conceivable Superman nightmare involving John Williams and people being upset with me no matter what I did. I really felt it was a 'damned if you do, damned if you don't' situation. I'm going to piss someone off no matter what I do. It was starting to cripple me.[10]

In the end, the movie itself was not a success at the box office or with Superman fans, but the score did receive critical acclaim from film-music critics and soundtrack enthusiasts.

When Zach Snyder set out to do his own version of Superman with 2013's *Man of Steel*, it would be the first film in what was to be known as the DC Extended Universe. Though directed by Snyder, the film was produced by Christopher Nolan, fresh off his successful DC Comics collaboration with Hans Zimmer on *The Dark Knight* trilogy, who recommended Zimmer as the composer for *Man of Steel*. As an extension of the DC world that Nolan and Zimmer created for *Dark Knight*, Synder wished for Zimmer to create a new type of score for his Superman movie that did not resemble the iconic John Williams score from 1978. As Sndyer continues:

> When Hans and I sat down and talked about what this music needs to be, the challenge with *Man of Steel* was that there was a score that had been written by John Williams for the 1978 Superman movie that was pretty powerful. And the challenge that I put to Hans was that we need to create a new experience for the audience, and the way that we've had to approach the whole movie was like, 'What if there was no Superman movie before?'[11]

Given the legacy of the John Williams score, Zimmer was not interested in being the film's composer, explaining that he told Synder:

> I don't think I can do Superman, I think John Williams is your man. John is, without a shadow of a doubt, the greatest living film composer, and he casts a large shadow. It's not about other people comparing us, it's my own insecurities comparing myself. Do I really want to put myself through this? This is an American icon, I think it needs to be an American that scores this film.[12]

After this initial reluctance, Zimmer went on to create a masterful and unique score for the film that was very different than John Williams' earlier and more traditional orchestral approach. Zimmer innovatively used a section of lap steel guitar players, 12 drummers, and commissioned original metal musical sculptures that could be performed for the score along with electronics and orchestra on the final score. Zimmer also worked with composer Junkie XL on some additional music for the film.

In 2016, Snyder went on to direct *Batman v Superman: Dawn of Justice* and asked Zimmer to compose the score. This was an additional challenge for Zimmer because he had already scored Christopher Nolan's *Dark Knight* trilogy, which starred Christian Bale as Batman, while Snyder's film had a new Batman in Ben Affleck. Zimmer explains the difficulty of not wanting to betray his earlier work with Nolan:

> For me, it was doubly daunting, because I've already done eleven years of Christian Bale as Chris Nolan's Batman and I didn't want to betray what I did in that time. I didn't want to go and belittle it, or say, 'Oh, this is all different, you know, forget about that, let's start again, in a casual way.[13]

The solution was for Zimmer to collaborate again with Junkie XL. Zimmer would revisit the themes he wrote for Superman in *Man of Steel*, while assigning Junkie XL to compose the new Batman theme for the Snyder film. Junkie XL explains the issues with the previous Nolan Batman legacy:

Hans had had a legacy to protect, a very impressive legacy with Christopher Nolan with Christian Bale. When Zach was going to take on Batman in this film, with a different Batman, Ben Affleck, the natural response of Hans was, it would be the best scenario for everybody, in respect to everybody, that we bring in another composer for the Batman side of things.[14]

With the success of both *Man of Steel* (2013) and *Batman v Superman* (2016), DC began developing more films for their DC Extended Universe, which included a series of Wonder Woman films. One of the consequences of the appearance of Wonder Woman in *Batman v Superman* was the need to create a Wonder Woman theme that could be used across all of her films which had not yet been written. Zimmer discusses:

We are expected to write a motif or something that can go and transcend a few years of movies, and you realize that there is this grand plan that we have to serve, and somehow make sure that over there, in three years' time, something we set up as a tiny, little minuscule motif resonates or pays off.[15]

Zimmer continues with the difficulty of finding the right theme for Wonder Woman:

We went through every cliche to try to find a sound for Wonder Woman. We did that tribal voices, we tortured every great singer, and suddenly I remember this phenomenal cellist Tina Guo who, when you meet her, is one of the most polite, articulate, feminine, sweet [people]. Then when she plays her electric cello standing up, when she grabs that cello, she grabs it like a sword and everything changes. You go, 'whoa, hang on a second,' and she wields that cello, like a weapon. And I thought, there it is, there she is, you know, she transforms. I wanted it to be a woman to make the banshee cry.[16]

Most franchises have multiple composers to score the various films. Occasionally, one composer will write the music for the entire franchise, such as Steve Jablonsky's work on *Transformers*, Howard Shore's music for *The Lord of the Rings* and *The Hobbit* films, Charlie Clouser's scoring in the *Saw* movies. It can often be the case in Hollywood that, when a film is successful, they bring in a new composer of higher professional status for the next films. Charlie Clouser expresses his gratitude for being allowed to compose for all the films in the *Saw* franchise:

I definitely feel lucky that they didn't all of a sudden call in a triple A-list composer to replace me for the second one. I think part of it is that the soundscapes that I created in the first couple were so left-field, that it would have sounded weird if they had slotted in 'a normal composer.' Maybe that composer would have been struggling to try to duplicate some of the weird, bowed metal sound effect type of stuff that I was doing. So it might have just been the path of least resistance to just keep me on.[17]

THE SERIES

The history of television series dates back to the late 1940s when TV sets started to appear in American households. The first regularly scheduled television series was *Texaco Star Theater*, which debuted in 1948 and was hosted by Milton Berle.

The show quickly became a hit and helped to popularize television as a form of entertainment.

Throughout the 1950s and 1960s, television series continued to grow in popularity, with shows like *I Love Lucy* (1951–1957), *The Honeymooners* (1955–1956), *The Twilight Zone* (1959–1964), and *Star Trek* (1966–1969) becoming cornerstones in American culture. These shows helped to establish many of the conventions of television storytelling that are still used today, such as the use of episodic structures, ensemble casts, and recurring characters.

In the 1970s and 1980s, television series continued to evolve, with shows like *M*A*S*H* (1972–1983), *All in the Family* (1971–1979), *The Mary Tyler Moore Show* (1970–1977), and *Hill Street Blues* (1981–1987) pushing the boundaries of what was possible in terms of storytelling and character development. These shows helped to establish the idea of television drama as a serious form of storytelling and paved the way for many of the more complex and ambitious series that would follow in the decades to come.

In the 1990s and 2000s, television series underwent a major transformation, with the rise of cable and then streaming services leading to a proliferation of new shows and new ways of telling stories. Shows like *The Sopranos* (1999–2007), *The Wire* (2002–2008), and *Breaking Bad* (2008–2013) helped to redefine what was possible in terms of the scope, complexity, and sophistication of television storytelling, and led to a new era of prestige television and streaming services.

One milestone in the synthesis of a long-story television-based format with theatrical production quality was the series *Lost* (2004–2010). Due to its large ensemble cast and the cost of filming primarily on location in Oahu, Hawaii, the series was one of the most expensive on television, with the pilot alone costing over $14 million – the most expensive pilot ever shot at that time.

Lost was a significant departure from traditional television production methods. The show's creators, J.J. Abrams, Damon Lindelof, and Jeffrey Lieber, wanted to create a cinematic quality for the show, which meant using high-quality 35mm cinema cameras, digital editing, and extensive post-production effects, including CGI, to create many of the show's fantastical elements.

One of the most important musical features of *Lost* was J.J. Abrams' insistence on an orchestral soundtrack for the show, composed by Michael Giacchino. Up to this time, most television shows were scored using synthesizers and a few live instruments, mainly due to budgetary constraints. TV scores tended to be mood and texture based, rather than the thematic way films were scored. As Giacchino explains:

> When I started working in TV, my fear was that I wasn't going to be able to work with a live orchestra because there were no shows that were using a live orchestra, because it's expensive, and over the years synthesizers have come to replace live musicians, which is very sad. So when I met J.J. [Abrams], one of our first conversations was that I felt like we had to do it with a live orchestra.[18]

The effect of both the show's success and the critical praise of the score helped usher in an age of long-form shows with cinematic orchestral scores. As production budgets grew, so did the diversity of the locations, the splendor of sets, the magnitude of special effects, and the cinematic richness of the musical scores.

Game of Thrones represents another important milestone in the expansion of the budget per episode. By its final season, HBO was spending $15 million per episode. With a larger music budget, *Game of Thrones* established the place of the orchestral score as a crucial element for a series, just like with a masterfully scored film. Of his filmic approach to *Game of Thrones*, composer Ramin Djawadi says:

> It was in the beginning, before I even started writing, I sat down with [showrunners] David and Dan, and we just discussed the tone of the show. We knew we wanted something different, we wanted to make sure we have our own style and our own tone. So we discussed instrumentation, a thematic approach, an orchestral score with interesting solo instruments.[19]

With every new hit series, individual episode budgets grow larger. In 2022, each individual episode of season four of *Stranger Things* cost $30 million, while the first season of *The Lord of the Rings: The Rings of Power* (2022–) cost $58 million dollars per episode, which is more than the entire budget of many major films. Many of these streamers feature cinematic orchestral scores, as heard in *Westworld*, *The Crown* (2016–2023), *The Mandalorian* (2019–), *Loki*, *Lord of the Rings: Rings of Power*, *House of the Dragon* (2022–), and *Andor* (2022–).

For the first time in history, we are seeing long-format storytelling of equal production value across film, television, streaming services, and video games. The length of content is also expanding: the entirety of *Breaking Bad* is 60 hours, *Game of Thrones* is over 70 total hours, and *Lost* exceeds 90 hours. If we include films and streaming series, the Marvel Cinematic Universe is 190 hours and counting, while the *Star Wars* universe is over 155 hours. What was once a single moment of time and a narrative captured in a single film, now spans generations of characters and eons of time.

We are seeing large franchises made up of film trilogies, streaming series, video games, and animated series. All modes of visual narrative storytelling seem to be converging into larger narrative universes, and it will be very exciting to see how the mediums of film, streaming series, and video games evolve in the near future, and what new approaches to scoring will emerge with them.

CHAPTER SUMMARY

- As cinema evolved, film lengths increased.
- The success of *Star Wars* ushered in the long-narrative form of the trilogy.
- Most trilogies use the same composer.
- The success of trilogies led to larger movie franchises like *Star Wars*, the Marvel Cinematic Universe, *Mission: Impossible*, and *The Lord of the Rings*.
- Larger movie franchises tend to use different composers for each film, but they often have franchise-brand musical themes like *James Bond*, *Mission: Impossible*, and *Star Wars*.

- In the early 2000s, digital editing, digital special effects, and the use of orchestral scores have increased the production value of television and streaming series making them competitive with theatrical films.
- The budgets of many streaming series episodes are equal to entire feature film budgets.

NOTES

1 Stefancos (2007, August 19). "John Williams Talks the Phantom Menace Part III". *YouTube*. https://www.youtube.com/watch?v=lUZmf68rzU8

2 Epicleff Media (2020, August 26). "Score: The Podcast S3E15 | Howard Shore: The King of the Rings". *YouTube*. https://www.youtube.com/watch?v=_anj3b8N3jE

3 Mix With the Masters (2020, July 18). "Writing to Picture With Hans Zimmer". *YouTube*. https://www.youtube.com/watch?v=sj2PdzPzyYY

4 Stefancos (2007, August 19). "John Williams Talks the Phantom Menace Part I". *YouTube*. https://www.youtube.com/watch?v=ZdYflV5-a2c

5 Larson, Randall D. (2013, August 27). "Danny Elfman on Scoring Mission: Impossible". Soundtrack!   https://cnmsarchive.wordpress.com/2013/08/27/danny-elfman-on-scoring-mission-impossible/#:~:text=Once%20the%20decision%20was%20made,that%20it%20would%20sound%20bigger

6 Magic Sounds and Music (2007, June 23). "Michael Giacchino Scoring Mission Impossible III". *YouTube*. https://www.youtube.com/watch?v=TrDOV9ZJVxE

7 Light The Fuse Podcast (2020, June 12). "104. Joe Kraemer Interview, Part 1 (Composer of 'Mission: Impossible – Rogue Nation')". *YouTube*. https://www.youtube.com/watch?v=MKtqz6Vt8Xw

8 FilmSpeak (2018, July 28). "Lorne Balfe Interview | Mission: Impossible – Fallout". *YouTube*. https://www.youtube.com/watch?v=pITI6Abw_S4

9 *Ibid.*

10 Ain't it Cool News (2006, June 27). "ScoreKeeper Conversates With Supermand Returns Composer & Editor John Ottman!!". http://legacy.aintitcool.com/node/23712

11 Flashback FilmMaking (2018, Apr 25). "Zack Snyder about Hans Zimmer 'Man of Steel' Behind the Scenes". *YouTube*. https://www.youtube.com/watch?v=wI0IFZcrm5U

12 FSinterview (2013, June 14). "Hans Zimmer Interview – Man of Steel". *YouTube*. https://www.youtube.com/watch?v=dHvamU98GhA

13 Elegyscores (2016, March 18). "Hans Zimmer & Junkie XL – Batman v Superman Interview 2". *YouTube*. https://www.youtube.com/watch?v=1CIzz10hXvk

14 *Ibid.*

15 *Ibid.*

16 *Ibid.*

17 Film.Music.Media (2021, April 30). "All Access: Charlie Clouser". *YouTube*. https://www.youtube.com/watch?v=OVq8FKmiggE

18 Magic Sounds and Music (2007, June 23). "Michael Giacchino on scoring LOST". *YouTube*. https://www.youtube.com/watch?v=v1K4Fsk3rG8

19 ShowTime (2017, September 16). "Game of Thrones Q&A With composer Ramin Djawadi". *YouTube*. https://www.youtube.com/watch?v=Dz8dpvxW0mM

10

NEW VOICES IN FILM MUSIC

The Interviews

RACHEL PORTMAN

A veteran of the film–scoring world, British composer Rachel Portman made history in 1997 when she became the first female composer to win an Academy Award for her score in the period comedy *Emma*. In 2015, she also became the first female composer to win a Primetime Emmy Award for the HBO film *Bessie* (2015). She received two further Academy Nominations for *The Cider House Rules* (1999) and *Chocolat* (2000). In total, he has scored over a hundred films, television series, and plays, including *Mona Lisa Smile* (2003), *The Manchurian Candidate* (2004), and *The Duchess* (2008). In recognition of her contributions to the arts, Portman was named an Officer of the British Empire (OBE) in 2010.

In Rachel Portman's words:

> I think creativity is something unique. It's when a person makes up something, or thinks in a way, or writes something, or paints something, or models something which is new or individual in some way. It's taking something and interpreting it in a way that is really personal to them, in a way that other people see and are inspired by, which immediately imposes a judgment on it. Who do I think is creative? It's somebody who does something that makes me think 'Wow.' It can be in the eye of the beholder.
>
> You are a craftsman as a composer, whether you write film music, or whether you write music for the concert hall because your craft is your orchestration – it's all that sort of those years of learning. And particularly for film music, it's very important to know that it is a craft. You're serving a film, you're not serving yourself, but there is an enormous amount of original creativity within that. When it works, it's a fantastic alchemy, and so often it doesn't work, because it's all craft, and no originality or creativity. Or it's all creativity but it's not grounded or rooted in actuality. This is a job where you are always hoping for a healthy collaboration with a director, but quite often it's like, 'Do this, do that, do this.' You're serving the film, you're always thinking of the interests of the film, and you've got the director and producers voicing opinions on what you're doing. So it's a strange thing.

DOI: 10.4324/9781003289722-10

Over the years, I have had to fight for things that I think are right. In the days when you didn't have these demos that have to be so beautifully programmed, there was much more of a mystery about what film composers do, and with that came more respect. And, I hesitate to say, as this isn't always the case, there are directors who you work with who are like, 'No, we defer to you, you know, you know what you're doing,' but there has been a tendency for everyone to pile in and say, 'Well, I don't like that' or 'Don't do this' or 'Do that.'

The craft of the composer can be sort of . . . abused is too strong a word, but taken for granted. Everyone who's worked on a film knows that there are these films that we just have to endlessly redo. You redo things again and again and again, because for some reason they're not liking what you do, and you've creatively run dry. In other films I've been pushed by the director to go back and redo a lot of stuff, and the music's gotten a lot better, because I've dug deeper, and it's been a really positive thing.

I like writing on pencil and paper, and I still do. I haven't made the transition to write in any other way, so I'm very low-tech. My composition is born out of classical education, and so when I do work on projects that need to have samples, I work with a programmer for that. I'm lucky because there's no way I could set myself up as a film composer today, without being able to do all my own demos with samples. However, I notice that a lot of [other composers'] compositions start from samples – it starts from searching for a sound – whereas mine start from the musical idea, always. I think that is a big shift that I've noticed working with people who write in a completely different way from me. So [for them] it's about pulling in things from here and there, whereas I'm starting and waiting for some kind of inspiration, which is normally melodic or harmonic, that exists on the page in notes that I write with a pencil on manuscript paper. A lot of composers and programmers don't work with notation. I feel very lucky to be able to get away with the way I write, and it's only because I've been doing it for so long that I'm able to.

I work at a piano. I would say it's mostly in my head, and the piano is there as a friend. Otherwise, it's really quiet. So I'm mostly having musical thoughts and I think writing music is a very unconscious thing. If you're trying too hard or if you're thinking too much about what or how you are doing it, it doesn't work. I often feel like I'm standing on the outside of something for quite a while. Even though I could tell you what I don't want to do, I haven't yet found what I do want to do. So I'm waiting for that idea to fall into my lap, and it's always worrying. Each time you think, 'I don't think I can do it this time, it's not gonna happen,' and the clock's ticking. I pity poor film composers because it's really hard.

I can't write a film score starting with the front titles and then going to the end. I look for the place in the film that speaks to me the most. Or I look for one or two places that are, for me, where the energy is, that will help me come up with a voice. And then when I feel I've got something that feels right to me, I work out from there. I usually write the front titles last because they should be the essence of one of the places that I've got from the middle of the film.

I watch a lot of films, but I don't listen to film music. In fact, I find it really difficult listening to film music. When I'm watching films, it's like there's one ear out to what the composer is doing and I'm missing huge amounts of plot going on. I've never formally studied anything properly. I've never studied a film score. I might have enjoyed one and thought, 'Oh, that's really cool.' We're all sponges influenced by everything. But I haven't ever, including when I was young and starting out, studied the greats or listened to what they did. I just went to the movies because I liked them. So my formative education in writing music for film was really, more than anything, about thinking about drama and film, and what worked, and getting an instinct for how drama works. I knew the music bit that I wanted to do, so it was about getting experience in putting music against drama.

KRIS BOWERS

Kris Bowers is an award-winning film-score composer and pianist known for his thought-provoking, genre-defying film compositions that pay homage to his classical and jazz roots. Bowers has composed music for film, television, and video games, while collaborating with the likes of Jay-Z, Kanye West, Kobe Bryant, Mahershala Ali, Justin Simien, and Ava DuVernay. His works include *The Snowy Day* (for which he won the Daytime Emmy Award in 2017), *Dear White People* (2014–2021), *Green Book* (2018), *When They See Us* (2019), *Black Monday* (2019–2021), *Madden NFL 20*, *Mrs. America* (2020), *Bridgerton*, *Bad Hair* (2020), *The United States vs. Billie Holiday* (2021), *Space Jam: A New Legacy* (2021), *Respect* (2021), and *King Richard* (2021). In 2020, Bowers also co-directed the documentary short film *A Concerto is a Conversation* with filmmaker Ben Proudfoot. Executive produced by Ava DuVernay, the film premiered at the 2021 Sundance Film Festival and was nominated for Best Documentary (Short Subject) at the 93rd Academy Awards.

In Kris Bowers' words:

Creativity, in general, is the expression of feeling through any particular medium. Essentially, creativity is informed by the processes that you've been exposed to, have practiced, or feel most comfortable in. But really, it's just how we express our inner being through some sort of form. Craftsmanship to me feels like the technique side of how to express that creativity. So with composition, for example, understanding orchestration techniques feels like the craftsmanship side, but how you use those techniques is creativity.

The craftsmanship side comes mostly through teachers, or through studying books and any literature that can be found, but also studying aurally. Especially with film scoring, there aren't many scores that you can go look at, but you can definitely listen to things and transcribe how they are orchestrated. On the creativity side, I feel like there are no rules for how that can be developed. I'm thinking about the fact that there are so many times that I'm inspired by a composer who maybe doesn't have the same depth of craftsmanship as somebody else, but their expression through that form, that medium, is so unique and inspiring because of how creative they are. I always go back to the blues, just the fact that blues musicians are incredibly creative, even if their craftsmanship was not as high as other musicians, or technical as other musicians. So I feel like the creative part of it is developed through life.

I still like writing things on the page because I'm pretty visual, especially with themes. If I'm writing a theme, I usually write the theme out visually, just because then I can assess, 'Are there any rhythms I want to use from this to continue to build on that thematically? Are there any sections from this theme that I can break down and use as motivic pieces?' But other than that, a lot of my orchestration I do in the box [computer], where I'll have my template set up. And I'll get the bass movement and the melody going, mock those up, and then a lot of the inner lines are just record and improvise, essentially. Then I'll go back and adjust the MIDI to what I want it to be. And then I'll do that for both of the inner lines so then I can always go back and say, 'Okay, I don't really like that movement between those two voices, let me make these adjustments.'

I feel like ever since I started composing in Logic [computer DAW] and became a film composer, I no longer was fully orchestrating with pencil and pad, and for me it's nice. I mean, it's kind of a crutch because I feel like you get to hear it, and you can hear all those things working in real time.

Going back to what I said about craftsmanship and creativity, I just did this masterclass and I played them some music from this Marvel show, and they were like, 'It sounds cool, but it also sounds like a Marvel thing. How do you have your own voice in those things?' I think for me, I've always approached it slightly differently. I always think about it the way that I thought about the jazz process, where if I'm playing Louis Armstrong, I want to improvise in a specific way, if I'm playing '50s stuff, I'm gonna have to improvise in a specific way, or if I'm playing something more modern. So I always wanted to really work hard to figure out how to improvise within the idiom, and I feel like, as a composer, that feels really exciting to me too – to be able to write for this fantasy adventure thing while also being able to write for some sort of indie, obscure thing. I have studied a lot of different stuff for that reason.

I'm definitely always studying, and I always use my jobs as reasons to study more. I usually say yes to things when I feel like they're going to challenge me as a composer and make me excited about what I'll be studying. In every project, I'm always comparing myself to my favorite artists, my favorite composers, and my favorite scores. Right now I'm working on a Marvel show, and I wanted to do this show because of the limited experience I have writing for big action things. Then, at the same time, the production aspect is something that I feel like I'm still learning, and so a lot of my process working on this has been studying other things to see what other tools I can develop.

John Williams has always been the person I go to, even if I'm writing stuff that doesn't seem obvious to him. I'm always fascinated by how he used orchestration or harmony to evoke a certain emotion. And so oftentimes I'll just go to him to get something that feels eerie, or nostalgic, or warm or any specific feeling, and then I try to borrow that harmonic approach and see if it can inform whatever I'm doing. I usually create a playlist for each project that I'm working on and fill that playlist with music that feels like it's kind of inspiring me in that space. So film score composers-wise, I would say John Williams, Bernard Herrmann, and John Powell. On the production side, Hans Zimmer every now and then, and then it's a lot of classical composers like Stravinsky . . . a lot of Tchaikovsky lately . . . I really love Brahms, Ravel, and Debussy. Those are the ones that I often come back to.

I'm also very inspired by somebody like Jonny Greenwood, or Mica Levi, or Hildur Guðnadóttir, all of whom, if they were scoring a Marvel movie, it would not sound like any Marvel movie you've ever heard before. I think they have a mastery of craftsmanship that is very particularly suited to their creative voice. And so I encourage people to really be curious and honest about whatever their creative voice is based on, what they're inspired by, the creations that they've made, and then to really be obsessed with pursuing how to perfect and master your craft as it relates to that creative voice.

PINAR TOPRAK

Pinar Toprak is an Emmy-nominated composer, conductor, and performer with an unmatched gift for creating memorable thematic scores for everything from superhero sagas and blockbuster comedies to TV dramas. With her work on *Captain Marvel* and *Fortnite*, she is the first female composer to score both a film and video game with gross revenues of over $1 billion and $5 billion respectively. Pinar's diverse body of work also includes the scores for *The Lost City* (2022), *Shotgun Wedding* (2022), *Slumberland* (2022), *Stargirl* (2020–2022), *Krypton* (2018–2019), and *McMillions* (2020).

In Pinar Toprak's words:

This is how I see creativity when it relates to music or what I do. I always feel that first you need to feel, then you need to be able to hear, and then, lastly, it's your knowledge of your craft that is able to translate those feelings and what you're hearing in your head, either down on paper, or computer, or whatever the medium you use. So it's a tool.

When you're learning something, if you have 100 words, the language that you know, what you can describe, what you can articulate, is limited to those words. The larger your vocabulary is, which is your craftsmanship, the easier it gets to be able to express those finer details of what you're feeling and what you're hearing. It makes some things easier, and some things more difficult. But it's ultimately, for me, that translation of feeling and hearing to creating.

The learning part almost feels like vacation to me. It's almost meditative for me to learn a new software, read a manual, or check out some video tutorials. I love learning and that's a part of my day, almost every day. It doesn't have to be a big chunk of anything. I think we overwhelm ourselves with all the things that we have to do in a day, but it can be quite minimal, really. Some days obviously are a bit more difficult than others, but for me that's part of the joy of learning. I always have this way of thinking that what I know is not the best way. I'm always like, 'I bet there are people doing it better than I'm doing right now. What is that way?' It's always this addiction to optimization and productivity, which I think provides the groundwork to evolve constantly. There's always a bit of dissatisfaction that's built into that, but I think that's being an artist.

I love studying scores, and I revisit scores that I've loved. When I was getting my master's 20 years ago, the mindset I had and what I was paying attention to was very different than what I pay attention to now. So even if it's the same thing I've studied before, I still discover something new with score study and technology. I mean, YouTube is fantastic. There are so many tutorial videos in there with people that are posting tips and tricks.

The score study thing really happens for me with classical repertoire. When it comes to current music, there's a different kind of brain that I sometimes activate, because if I listen to a lot of other soundtracks all the time, that's not really productive to what I'm doing. But nonetheless, what we're doing is we're creative, but we're also a business and it is basic market research. You need to be aware of what other people are currently doing because those things come up in conversations. A director or producer or studio will say, 'Oh, we want something along the lines of this and this,' so it's good to be able to know what's going on currently in your line of business.

In terms of composition and orchestration, the score study part is, just for me, a lot more classical repertoire based. I really do love Mahler, I love Elgar, I love a lot of Tchaikovsky, I love Debussy, and Ravel. I think there are certain things that I don't know in orchestration – you realize that the more you dive into something – and it's kind of overwhelming. The more I learn, the less I know, and that's kind of frustrating because it's almost like it's better to be ignorant and not know what you don't know. There are a lot of people on this earth that live like that. I'm very envious of them, but for me, I don't live in that state of mind.

If I need to create something, if I have an assignment to do, I'm not in that meditative study mindset. So I do all the studying and having fun learning things when the pressure is a bit low. And those things kind of stay in the background. I remember when I was learning all the figured bass stuff and when I had to write fugues and things, I'm like, 'I'm not gonna write fugues.' But then I started realizing how it becomes second nature. It's the same thing when I try to study something, I let it kind of be a part of me and hope that it comes out when it needs to.

The tricky thing is that everything is important. It's not just one thing. It's really about getting better at technology, using the tools that you have, because now we need to do things so fast, and so knowing your tools is really important. Being able to deliver, and benchmarking your stress and your technology, just so that when you do get the call or an email, that you're able to produce something in a timely fashion. I think that's a really good skill set to generally work on. These are all things that everybody should know, just the musicianship and the tech side of it.

I start on the piano if it's a score that needs to have a tune. Some scores are a lot more sound design, texture, synths, and things, which are a bit different. But if it's a kind of score that needs that tune, or more than one tune – the main theme – that's where I start first because that unlocks a lot of things, and how I write that tune changes whether it's on the piano. A lot of times, I just walk and I start humming to myself. Walking, to me, unlocks a lot of things. I find it very meditative. I always think that if you can hum it, if you can easily sing something, then it's good and accessible to people in the audience, and it can connect with people.

It usually starts with finding the tune, whether I'm singing it or playing it on the piano. And from there I write a basic sketch. It could be just strings and piano or something. I'm just trying to outline harmonically and tempo-wise, and find the zip code of where I want to be. Then a lot of times I write suites – that's how I've been getting the sound palette. I think it helps solve a lot of issues that might come along the way with the filmmakers because if you have a suite, everyone knows the sonic world that we live in; you know, this is the harmonic language, these are the tunes in this order, the general instrumentation, so nothing comes as a shock when they hear a new cue. This is our world. I find that usually, my next step from there is individual cues, one cue at a time.

There's not really a locked picture anymore. I don't think I've worked on the lock picture for a long time. I've been brought on with a rough cut, with a director's cut, with nothing shot whatsoever, at the script stage. It's really all varied. With some filmmakers you know what they're going to make if you have a relationship built. But then a lot of films change quite a bit from script to what it ends up being, so it varies.

As a film composer, or media composer, I never thought of myself as in the music industry. I always felt that I was working in the film industry and my position was in the music department. So with that said, you need to know about filmmaking, you need to watch films, and you need to understand what it takes to get a film made, so that when you are having a conversation with a director, you're able to understand where they're coming from, because a lot of times composers take things personally, but it's not. They've been living and breathing this film for so long, and after all the ordeals they have overcome, they come to you in the final stages to do score, and I try to come from that compassion, and understanding it's really difficult to get a film made, forget about a big one. It's really, really difficult to get a film made.

I'm in love with films. I feel like I'm more in love with films than I'm in love with music sometimes. I love storytelling. Of course, I pay attention to the music but it's really the medium. These days there are a lot of really great films being made, but in addition to films, video games have gotten insanely great as well. Limited series, for example. For me, that's so satisfying, because you don't have like six seasons to watch, but you have eight episodes, ten episodes where it's like a really well-explored film over a long period of time. I really love storytelling and all the emotions. Whether it's sci-fi or drama or action or comedy, there's heart and reason or logic, and all of these things are what fascinate me.

NATALIE HOLT

Natalie Holt is an award-winning British composer, known for her two-time Emmy-nominated score for Marvel Studios' *Loki* and the acclaimed Star Wars series *Obi-Wan Kenobi* (2022). Her long list of film and television credits include *Wallander* (2008–2016), *Knightfall* (2017–2019), *Three Girls* (2017), *Deadwater Fell* (2020), *The Honourable Woman* (2014), *Victoria* (2016–2019), *Journey's End* (2017), *Fever Dream* (2021), and *The Princess* (2022). Her numerous awards nominations and wins include the Primetime Emmy Awards, World Soundtrack Awards' "Television Composer of the Year," BAFTA, SCL Awards, the Royal Television Society Craft and Design Award, the HMMAs, and "Best International Score" at the Beijing International Film Festival.

In Natalie Holt's words:

> There are days when you feel just like you're doing something that is a job and a task, and it doesn't flow. I always feel like creativity happens when you get into this zone where you're one with what you're working on, and you're in the middle of an idea and you lose the sense of time. That's when I find I come up with an idea that I think, 'Oh, that's different from what I've been asked for,' but it's something I've created that's not just uniform or fitting into a mold of something. You've gone beyond and you've done something that you feel is new.
>
> If you talk of the craft as being your tools that you're creating with, I just find that, for me, it's like a connection between the piano and the violin and the image. If I'm thinking about, 'Oh, I need to program this,' or 'I'm kind of getting lost in the technology,' or 'Oh, I need to change the way my sample library is set up,' it's sort of mundane, like cleaning your house or something. You can get lost in programming samples to sound like real violins, and that in itself is a different job away from composing. So for me, it's important to keep those pure connections where you're not thinking about the interface, and it's just you and the image and the music.
>
> Some directors feel like they understand every part of the filmmaking process, but music is like a foreign language and it's something that they find very confusing. With those directors, you tend to have to program things as if it's going to be a finished product. But I spoke to Danny Elfman about this recently and he said whenever he gets a director who he hasn't worked with before, he'll get them to come into his studio and he'll say, 'Look, this is a sketch,' and he'll play it to them. Then he'll say, 'This is how it turned out once I've recorded it with the orchestra.' And then he says, 'So trust me, I've done this. This is just an idea so you have to understand this, and if you get caught in all of this, then we won't get anywhere.' If you're Danny Elfman, you can do that, can't you?
>
> I watch the picture and I'll just create a piano sketch of everything mapped out, so I can hear it in my head and not get bogged down with programming. Most of my scores have got a kind of hybrid quality to them. I've been working on really big superhero things that have needed that big scale, but it would be really nice to go back and do something smaller, which is just live instruments again. I love the journey of having a contrast in projects.
>
> If I've got a gestation period before I need to deliver things to picture, then I'll sit at the piano and just make sure I'm coming up with really durable themes, and thematic underpinning for the whole project. Then if I've got an idea of like, 'Oh, it would be really cool to do something with an unusual instrument,' then I'll try and go away and have a recording session with the instrument so I can have some of the colors there as well in the demos.

When I was coming up, I was delivering the whole thing and I'd have to mix it. It would be low budget, so you just do the whole thing with samples and if you have a few instruments, then mix and deliver. When I listen back to those times I'm like, 'Jesus, this sounds dreadful,' and I think, 'No, I'm not an engineer.' I don't think I've got the best sense of it. I'll over-mix something and bring out weird things, or I'll just make it sound like mush. I've worked with [mix engineer] Jake Jackson for the last few years and he's so fantastic. I tried working with engineers, and it's very difficult finding the right person. It's like a relationship. They have respected the idea that you've started, but then they'll just elevate it and that's how I see orchestrators or engineers. Very often, if you're bogged down in a cue, and you're tired, it's nice for someone else to do it. Then you get it back and you can have an overview of it. It's like keeping that perspective. I feel like it's really important, and it's a luxury because in order to get to this place, you have to be a one-man band for a certain period of time.

I didn't feel like I could fit in with my own voice as a concert composer. And for some reason, film music felt to me like the way forward. That's where it's happening, merging music with these other art forms. If you ask me to write a piece away from a story, I can't. I don't see the point of it in a way. I had this ability to deeply connect with the character or understand the emotion that the director was trying to do, or what the music should say. I watched a blank scene and I would just hear, 'Oh, it needs to sound like that.'

I'm a huge movie lover. My idea of a treat is getting a pass for a film festival and then just going, 'Oh, that sounds interesting.' I love going to Cannes and London Film Festival. I watched about four movies a day. I do listen to soundtracks as well. I find myself listening to lots of podcasts with composers talking about things as well. It's interesting just hearing how people work and keeping inspired as well, and not running out of steam with it.

GLOSSARY OF TERMS

Anempathetic Music A type of music that does not express the feeling or emotion of the scene, which leads to a perceptual disconnect between what we see and what we hear, such as comical music that plays during a frightening scene.

CGI Computer Generated Imagery is a technique using computer software to generate and manipulate images for realistic special effects.

Cinematic In video games, a short non-interactive movie that plays to advance the plot, introduce new characters, provide exposition, or add emotional impact to important moments in the game.

Cinematographe A hand-cranked mechanism pioneered by the Lumière brothers, where film is advanced through the camera and projector, which employs a shutter mechanism to create the illusion of motion.

Cutscene In video games, a type of cinematic (see above) shown to the player when they reach a particular point in the game, such as at the end of a level where the scene finishes automatically while the player is still in active gameplay mode.

DAW A Digital Audio Workstation is a computer software application used for recording, editing, and producing audio files.

Diegetic Music A term used to describe music that comes from the world of the film, also known as *source music*. Songs that are heard by the characters in a film, such as music playing on a car radio, are an example of diegetic music.

Dolby Theater Sound A sound system developed by Dolby Laboratories for movie theaters, designed to provide high-quality sound reproduction that is optimized for the movie theater environment, creating a more immersive and realistic audio experience for moviegoers.

Dub Stage The phase of production where the final sound mix of the film will be completed by the re-recording mixers.

Empathetic Music A type of music that directly expresses the feeling or emotion of the scene, such as sad music that plays during a sad scene or exciting music during an action chase.

Kinetophone A film projection device invented by Thomas Edison in the late 1800s that combined a kinetoscope – a projector displaying moving images on a screen – with a phonograph played the corresponding audio track.

Leitmotif A recurring musical theme that becomes associated with a character, place, or idea.

Loop A short section of music that is designed to repeat seamlessly, creating a continuous and repetitive pattern.

Metadiegetic Music A term used to describe music that can only be heard by a particular character or characters in the film.

Mickey Mousing A compositional technique involving the creation of music that mimics or reflects the movements of the characters or objects on screen, often through the use of musical accents. For example, if a character is walking, the music might include a series of rhythmic, marching sounds that correspond to the character's footsteps.

Middleware In video games, a type of program that sits between the game engine and the sound files for the game, and mediates between the behavior of the player in the environment and the appropriate sound which that behavior triggers.

MIDI A Musical Instrument Digital Interface is a technical standard used in electronic music devices to allow electronic music instruments, such as synthesizers, drum machines, and digital pianos, to communicate with computers and each other.

Mockup An extensive demo of a project built using virtual instrument software or hardware to stand in for acoustic instruments.

Non-diegetic Music A term used to describe music that only we, as the audience, can hear, such as the musical score.

Pre-production The planning and preparation stage before the actual filming begins, which includes financing, budgeting, script development, location scouting, casting, and set design.

Post-production The final stage of filmmaking that takes place after principal photography, which includes editing, visual effects, sound design, and music composition.

Optical Sound A film and sound recording technology where a separate track of sound could be recorded alongside the image on the filmstrip, allowing for higher quality sound and improved synchronization between the sound and image.

Ostinato A term used in music to describe a repeated pattern of notes or chords that is used as a foundation for a composition or section of a composition.

Sampler An electronic or digital musical instrument that uses sound recordings, or *samples*, of real instrument sounds that can be performed and modified using a keyboard or computer.

Spotting A process where a composer and director will sit and watch a rough cut of the film in order to decide which scenes will require music and which will not.

Stem A group of audio tracks that have been mixed together and exported as a single audio file. Stems are usually created by grouping together similar tracks, such as all the drums, all the guitar, or all the vocals.

Synthesizer An electronic musical instrument, typically operated by a keyboard, that electronically generates and modifies sound.

Temp Music A pre-existing piece of music that is temporarily put into the film before original music can be written, to serve as a guideline for the tempo, mood, or atmosphere the director is looking for in a scene.

Timbre A parameter of sound also known as tone color, timbre is a term used to describe the quality and character of a sound or musical note.

Vitaphone A sound-on-disc system developed by the Western Electric and Bell Telephone Laboratories in the late 1920s. It was one of the first practical methods of adding synchronized sound to motion pictures, and it revolutionized the film industry by introducing the era of "talkies."

Zoopraxiscope An early motion picture projector invented by Eadweard Muybridge in the 1870s.

SELECTED BIBLIOGRAPHY

FILM MUSIC PODCAST AND RADIO

Screen Sounds with Dan Golding. www.abc.net.au/classic/programs/screen-sounds
Art of the Score. www.artofthescore.com.au/
comPosers The Movie Score Podcast. https://composerspod.com/
The Film Scorer Podcast. https://thefilmscorer.com/the-film-scorer-podcast/
Score the Podcast. https://podcasts.apple.com/au/podcast/score-the-podcast/id1357882784
Settling the Score. www.settlingthescorepodcast.com/

FILM MUSIC YOUTUBE CHANNELS

COMPOSERS INTERVIEWS

Film Music Media Interviews. www.youtube.com/@FilmMusicMedia
Score: the Podcast. www.youtube.com/@EpicleffMedia

VIDEO ESSAYS

Dan Golding. www.youtube.com/@DanGoldingVideoEssays
Listening in. www.youtube.com/@ListeningIn
Sideways. www.youtube.com/@Sideways440/videos

FILM MUSIC ANALYSIS

Film Score Analysis with Brad Frey. www.youtube.com/@bradfrey
Film Score Analysis with David McCaulley. www.youtube.com/@DavidMcCaulley

ONLINE COURSES

Berklee Online Film Scoring. https://online.berklee.edu/courses/film-scoring-101
Danny Elfman Teaches Music for Film. www.masterclass.com/classes/danny-elfman-teaches-music-for-film
Film Scoring. www.udemy.com/course/film-scoring/

Hans Zimmer Teaches Film Scoring. www.masterclass.com/classes/hans-zimmer-teaches-film-scoring

Intro to Scoring for Film. https://soundfly.com/courses/intro-to-scoring-for-film-and-tv?gclid=CjwKCAjw5dqgBhBNEiwA7PryaO95Fn4XtPgLwB7GXZXFofnYvSdnVRuQa_pHGOkc-2LXm2Bo8YJ9ghoC2ogQAvD_BwE

BOOKS ON FILM SCORING AND FILM MUSIC

Bellis, Richard (2007). *The Emerging Film Composer*. https://www.amazon.com.au/Emerging-Film-Composer-Introduction-Psychology/dp/0615136230?asin=B005GMJ4CC&revisionId=51248be9&format=1&depth=1

Borum, Jeremy (2015). *Guerilla Film Scoring: Practical Advice from Hollywood Composers*. Rowman & Little.

Buhler, James and David Neumeyer (2015). *Hearing the Movies: Music and Sound in Film History*, 2nd Edition. Oxford University Press.

Chion, Michel (1990). *Audio-Vision*. Columbia University Press.

Cooke, Mervyn (2008). *A History of Film Music*. Cambridge University Press.

Davis, Richard (2010). *Complete Guide to Film Scoring: The Art and Business of Writing Music for Movies and TV*. Berklee Press.

Gorbman, Claudia (1987). *Unheard Melodies: Narrative Film Music*. Indiana University Press.

Kalinak, Kathryn (1992). *Settling the Score: Music and the Classical Hollywood Film*. University of Wisconsin Press.

Kalinak, Kathryn (2010). *Film Music: A Very Short Introduction*. Oxford University Press.

Mancini, Henry (1993). *Sounds and Scores: A Practical Guide to Professional Orchestration*. Alfred Music.

Music & Cinema (2000), edited by James Buhler, Caryl Flynn, and David Neumeyer. Wesleyan University Press.

Pendergast, Roy M. (1992). *Film Music: A Neglected Art*. W.W. Norton.

Rona, Jeff (2009). *The Reel World: Scoring for Pictures*. Hal Leonard.

Schifrin, Lalo (2011). *Music Composition for Film and Television*. Berklee Press.

Wierzbicki, James (2009). *Film Music: A History*. Routledge.

Wright, Rayburn (2013). *On the Track: A Guide to Contemporary Film Scoring*. Routledge.

DVD

Score: A Film Music Documentary, Epicleff Media

RECOMMENDED LISTENING

MAX STEINER

King Kong (1933)
Gone With the Wind (1939)
Casablanca (1942)

BERNARD HERRMANN

Vertigo (1958)
North by Northwest (1959)
Psycho (1960)

JERRY GOLDSMITH

Planet of the Apes (1968)
The Omen (1976)
Alien (1979)

ENNIO MORRICONE

The Dollars Trilogy (1964–1966)
The Mission (1986)
Cinema Paradiso (1988)

JOHN WILLIAMS

Jaws (1975)
Star Wars (1977)
E.T. The Extra-Terrestrial (1982)

HANS ZIMMER

Gladiator (2000)
Pirates of the Caribbean: At Worlds End (2007)
Inception (2010)

JOHN POWELL

Jason Bourne Trilogy (2002–2016)
Ice Age (2002–2012)
How to Train Your Dragon (2010–2019)

HARRY GREGSON-WILLIAMS

Man on Fire (2004)
Chronicles of Narnia (2005–2008)
The Last Duel (2021)

TRENT REZNOR

The Social Network (2010)
Girl with the Dragon Tattoo (2011)
Soul (2020)

JÓHAN JOHANNSON

Prisoners (2013)
Sicario (2015)
Arrival (2016)

MICA LEVI

Under the Skin (2013)
Jackie (2016)
Marjorie Prime (2017)

HILDUR GUÐNADÓTTIR

Sicario: Day of the Soldado (2018)
Chernobyl (2019)
Joker (2019)

INDEX

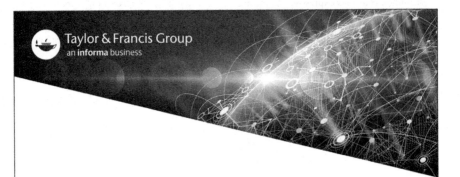

Printed in the United States
by Baker & Taylor Publisher Services